Babe Didrikson

Babe
Didrikson

THE GREATEST ALL-SPORT ATHLETE OF ALL TIME

Susan E. Cayleff

Foreword by Susan Stamberg

CONARI PRESS
Berkeley, California

Photographs courtesy of: 1). Mary and John Gray Library Special Collections, Lamar University, Beaumont, Texas, Document 11.2.22.1. 2). Gray/Collections, Document 11.2.22.8. 3). United States Olympic Committee Photo Library, Denver, Colorado. 4). Gray/Collections, Document 11.2.23.1. 5). Gray/Collections, no number. 6). Gray/Collections, no number. 7). Gray/Collections Document, 11.2.24.25. 8). Gray/Collections, Document 11.2.26.10.

Conari Press books are distributed by Publishers Group West.

ISBN: 1-57324-194-6

Cover and Book Design: Suzanne Albertson
Cover Art Direction: Ame Beanland
Cover Photography: Courtesy of Archive Photos

Library of Congress Cataloging-in-Publication Data

Cayleff, Susan E., 1954–
    Babe Didrikson : the greatest all-sport athlete of all time / Susan E. Cayleff ; foreword by Susan Stamberg.
        p.   cm. (The Barnard biography series)
    Includes bibliographical reference and index.
    Summary: A biography of Babe Didrikson, who broke records in golf, track and field, and other sports, at a time when there were few opportunities for female athletes.
    ISBN 1-57324-194-6 (pbk.)
    1. Zaharias, Babe Didrikson, 1911–1956—Juvenile literature.
2. Athletes—United States—Biography—Juvenile literature. 3. Women athletes—United States—Biography—Juvenile literature. [1. Zaharias, Babe Didrikson, 1911–1956. 2. Athletes. 3. Women—Biography.]
    I. Title. II. Barnard biography series (Berkeley, Calif.)

    GV697.Z26 C29 2000

To my family, Nathan, Fritzie,
and Joani Cayleff

and

Sue Gonda

I don't see any point in playing if I don't win. Do you?

—Babe Didrikson,
said repeatedly throughout her lifetime

Babe Didrikson

FOREWORD

Susan Stamberg, author of *TALK:*
NPR's Susan Stamberg Considers All Things

Babe Didrikson grew up in the Age of the Good Girl. And what an age it was! Girls ("young ladies") were expected to be modest, self-effacing, soft-spoken, proper, polite. Ladylike. These expectations flourished throughout Babe's life—from 1911 when she was born, to 1956 when she died. But Babe Didrikson ignored, or flouted, or just plain didn't care about the expectations of others. She cared about only one thing: winning.

Years ago, on National Public Radio, novelist Lois Gould told me that in pre-feminist days (the Good Girl days) little boys were raised to play on teams. They understood that it took eleven kids to play football, and all eleven couldn't possibly be their best friends. Boys were also taught that they had a choice: either play only with your best friend, or play football. Little girls, then, raised in a smaller one-on-one universe in which best friends were absolutely central, never had the broader choice to make. So girls played by themselves, or with just a single friend. And they played small, solitary sports, such as skating, swimming.

Golf is a solitary sport. And Babe Didrikson was likely the greatest female golfer of all time. But she also played basketball, baseball, and football. And excelled at them, too. She was a most unusual little girl and woman.

Today we take female athletes for granted. We thrill to their accomplishments on soccer fields and basketball courts, in Olympic competitions. In Babe's day, women athletes were rarities. Serious athleticism was unladylike. Being competitive wasn't being a Good Girl. Babe Didrikson was as competitive as they come. She would walk into the women's locker room before a tournament and say, "All right, which one of you will take second?" She didn't make a lot of best friends that way. But she won medal after medal.

"My goal was to be the greatest athlete that ever lived," she wrote in her autobiography, *This Life I've Led.* Notice she didn't say "greatest *female* athlete." She never permitted her gender to impose limits on her ambition.

As Susan Cayleff makes clear in this biography, tough circumstances enabled Babe to become a sports star. It helped that she was poor, and the second youngest of seven children. And that she grew up in sweltering, pre-air-conditioned Texas. Parents didn't want all those children underfoot. Texas weather permitted the kids to go outside to play. And the deprivations of poverty gave Babe a kind of freedom that cossetted wealthier children didn't have. There was less supervision, little class-conscious correction of behavior and manners. A girl could be a tomboy, play rough physical games, show off, and not shock anybody. She could be a girl, plain and simple. She could be more than a Good Girl. She could be free. Which helped her grow up a champion.

Few people know the name Babe Didrikson these days. But when I was young, she was everywhere—all over the papers, the radio, early television. I hadn't seen women like her (I was a child of the '50s), and something about her made me uncomfortable. She wasn't "feminine" in the way we middle-class '50s children were expected to be. You could tell from the stories that she was flamboyant and brash. Even cocky. And there was something mannish in her manner. The journalism of the day alluded to that, but in those proper and careful times, the idea that a woman could love another woman was never discussed. Like the word *cancer*, it was whispered rather than confronted. Also, like cancer, it was dangerous. Homosexuals were seen as deviant. Their sexual practices were illegal. So Babe Didrikson got married to a wrestler named George Zaharias, who managed her career and pushed her relentlessly. In her later years, a Texas golfer named Betty Dodd was her constant companion. Betty was twenty years younger than Babe, and simply worshiped her. Theirs was the real marriage, but Babe stayed wedded to George to "keep up appearances"— a quintessentially '50s phrase. In this new century, when appearances have changed and Good Girls are merely quaint curiosities, love between two men, or two women remains taboo in many circles, including those of professional sports. Society at large is more knowledgeable, maybe even more understanding, but those who choose to spend their lives with members of the same sex often keep quiet so as not to jeopardize their careers.

Babe Didrikson was never a feminist. She didn't fight for sexual liberation or women's rights. But in her field she was a pioneer. She helped to found the Ladies Professional Golf Association, and revolutionized her sport—brought a power and smash to the game that hadn't been there before Babe. The "ladies" of her day were shocked. But Babe just grinned, and hit her golf balls.

As you about read her life, you may find her to be more admirable than likeable. But I think that's the heart of Babe

Didrikson's story. She was driven. Not to please, or to accommodate. But to succeed. She never took up a sport simply for the fun of it, or to stay fit and trim. She played only to win. Babe was a champion.

ONE

The "Texas Tomboy"
Captures National Headlines

On a sultry July afternoon in 1932, Babe Didrikson, glistening with sweat, grass stains on her satin shorts, sprinted across the low-cropped grass to where the judges awaited her. She had just set a world record by throwing a baseball more than 272 feet. When it finally came down out of the sky the crowd had gasped—then burst into cheers and wild applause. Two hundred and seventy-two feet! Babe pushed her bangs off her forehead, squinted, and punched her fists in the air. She felt loose, strong, in control.

She waved to the crowd and headed directly for the dirt track. There her five competitors in the 80-meter hurdles were stretching and crouching, awaiting the pistol shot to start the race. Babe dug her toes into the turf.

She was too excited to notice her fatigue. Her heart was pounding in her chest. She flexed her muscles and tried to relax her breathing. All the hours of grueling practice—the uphill runs when she felt her lungs would burst, the sprints that made her legs burn—were for this. Those memories only fueled her fierce determination. She truly believed she was unbeatable. Her sense of physical power intoxicated her. She had brought all of this desire with her onto the track.

She crouched down, using her toes and fingertips to balance her weight. At the gunshot, she surged forward, propelled by her own adrenaline. "It's just like hurdling the hedges on Doucette Street," she told herself as she leaped over each hurdle flawlessly. She bent her knee, just as she had practiced in her neighborhood to allow for the thick sharp foliage of the hedges. She kept this style today at the race, even though the wooden hurdles were narrow and smooth. Floating across the top, she gained the perfect rhythm. "Just one more hurdle."

Her chest broke the tape stretched across the finish line. The crowd's praise exploded in her ears. "Twelve point one seconds!" the announcer's voice boomed through the stadium. "A new world record!"

It was her fourth win in four events. "Four events to go." If only her mother, Hannah, and father, Olé, could be there to see her. "Mine Babe!" she heard her mother's soft voice. "Mine Babe! We are so proud of our girl!" Thinking about her mother's affectionate nickname, Babe smiled and turned toward the cluster of reporters.

Although she was of average size and weight—5 feet 6 inches and 140 pounds—there was nothing average about Babe's presence. Indeed, she seemed larger than life. She was lithe, muscular, and as quick with a quip as she was quick on her feet. Her chestnut hair was close-cropped, her bangs uneven, and her brown eyes piercing. She posed for photographers with her hands on her hips, square jaw thrust out confidently, her arms reenacting a throw. She playfully swatted reporters' arms, laughed often, and grabbed a pencil from one sports writer. "Make sure you quote me right!" she teased him.

Neither shy nor unassuming, she loved being the center of attention and regaled the reporters with tall tales and "Texas talk" that had them scribbling down her every word. She beamed as she spun yarns about foot-racing a mad bull in a local cow pasture. Sure, that's how she'd developed her speed and agility. She also said she ran alongside the train as it passed through town—and darn if she hadn't outrun it, too. She claimed she had not thrown the javelin much at all, but it came to her so naturally that she had set the world record when she first picked it up in 1930. She accomplished all this at the age of only nineteen, she assured the writers.

She was actually twenty-one. But she thought the world would view her as even more of a phenomenon if she were still a teenager. The reporters could not know that she had also been practicing javelin with grueling regularity. She worked the press like a skilled carnival pitchman lures spectators in to see sideshows.

Reporters immediately took notice of her unusual physical attributes. She was lithe, lean, and strong, and it was obvious that she was uninterested in feminine styles or mannerisms in clothing or gestures. There was no doubt about her origins, since she exaggerated her Texas accent, delivering one-liners with a broad twang. Her outgoing personality appealed to the reporters, who were always hungry for a good quote.

Most of all, the press was enthralled because Babe had come to Evanston as a one-woman team. It was a stunt her coach, Colonel McCombs, devised. For the past two years, she had been playing basketball for McCombs' Employer's Casualty Insurance Company in Dallas, Texas. Hired officially to do secretarial work, Babe winked when she told reporters, "I can type 180 words a minute." In reality, she was rarely asked to sit at a desk. She was a paid athlete who competed for Employer's Casualty in the popular national Women's Industrial League.

Babe had led that semipro basketball team to its second consecutive national championship. But at the close of the season, McCombs worried that his star was becoming restless. So he suggested she represent Employer's Casualty at the Amateur Athletic Union (AAU) National Championships by participating in every event—a one-woman team. This unheard-of ploy would publicize Babe and her employer simultaneously. Babe readily agreed. She loved the chance to show off her skills in diverse sports.

The stunt worked perfectly. Before the meet began, the announcer called out each competing team and each group ran onto the field, welcomed by the spectators' applause. When Babe's "team" was called, a reporter wrote, "She ran onto the field all alone, waving her arms wildly, carried along by the roar of the crowd." Babe was pitted all by herself against 250 outstanding women athletes on teams with as many as twenty members. The challenge seemed insurmountable. She entered eight of ten events. She had to scramble to get from one event to the next on time, and more than once, officials delayed starting so she could catch her breath. They also allowed her time to rest between events.

Before the afternoon was finished, she had accomplished what most would have thought impossible. By nightfall, she had won four of her eight events outright: the shot put (an Amateur Athletic Union and United States record); javelin toss (breaking her own world record); 80-meter hurdles (also bettering her own world record); and the broad jump. She tied for first place in the high jump (an AAU record) and placed fourth in the discus, even though it was not an event in which she normally competed. She had won six gold medals (including the 272-foot baseball throw world record) and had broken four world records. Her performance earned her thirty points. The second-place team, the Illinois Athletic Club, earned only twenty-two points.

It was an incredible record, one that the sporting press broadcast to the nation. In the space of three hours, Babe had catapulted from anonymity to superstardom. On that singular July afternoon in 1932, Babe adroitly demonstrated two lessons she had learned as a young girl. First, attention justifies storytelling. Second, practice without mercy and excellence will follow. For Babe, winning and attention were sweet and seductive rewards.

As she stood on the track surrounded by awed admirers, Babe realized she had always been right: her destiny was to be the greatest athlete who ever lived.

TWO

Texas: Living
between Two Worlds

Mildred Ella Didriksen was a rambunctious mischief-maker even as an infant. Her mother, Hannah, greeted her birth on June 26, 1911, with a mixture of joy and worry for her baby's future. She and her husband were poor Norwegian immigrants, and the birth of their sixth child seemed like it would only make hard times harder.

Mildred Ella's family was unlike most others in their working-class Port Arthur, Texas, neighborhood; 95 percent of those surrounding them were American-born. Most Norwegians who immigrated to the United States lived in ethnic enclaves in farming country, where they wore traditional clothing from their homeland, held on to their old-world religious beliefs, and relied upon extended family and

Norwegian friends. The Didriksens did almost none of these things.

Babe's mother, born Hannah Marie Olson, was the daughter of a Bergen, Norway, shoemaker. She was 5 feet 4 inches tall and blessed with the natural grace of a born athlete. As a girl in her homeland, Hannah had been a skilled skater and skier. When Babe had achieved fame, she liked to brag that her mother had been a champion. While that was a fanciful concoction, Hannah nevertheless was a gifted athlete in her youth.

Babe's father, Olé, (pronounced O-lay) was born in Oslo, Norway. Although his own father was a cabinetmaker by trade, Olé was too adventurous to follow immediately in his footsteps. As a young man, Olé signed on as a merchant seaman aboard transatlantic oil tankers. Olé was tall and lean, with dark hair that framed his ruggedly handsome face. His drooping mustache added a rakish touch to his looks.

Babe never tired of hearing her father spin yarns about his life. Her earliest memories were of sitting cross-legged on the floor of their rambling, paint-chipped house in Port Arthur, transfixed by Olé's voice inflections and dramatic hand gestures. They could rarely afford paid entertainment. Nighttime storytelling was a family ritual and an art to be mastered. Babe clearly remembered her father's yarns and the hushed audience he commanded with exotic tales.

In her autobiography, *This Life I've Led,* Babe detailed her love of his stories. "He'd describe one trip where they got stranded on an island," Babe recalled. They "kept themselves alive by eating monkeys and things." In another favorite tale, which she begged him to retell time and again, "his ship broke up in a storm and he clung to a rope by one hand for hours, holding another guy up with his other hand." She adored his tales of derring-do and heroism. "What a bang we used to get out of his stories.... We'd huddle around him and listen like mad.... It could all be true. Things like that happened to these old seafarers."

Those stories made him a hero in his children's eyes, even though he was frequently unemployed. He placed himself at the center of every story. He crafted an image of himself as a footloose, roguish adventurer who scratched out a living in the rough and unpredictable working-class realm of the waterfront.

The Didriksens, like many other Norwegians, cherished storytelling—often more so than book knowledge. Entertaining a rapt audience with vivid and graphic detail allowed you to control your listeners at "tongue's end." No harm was done if the tale was exaggerated. It was most important to satisfy yourself and your listeners. This lesson Babe embraced as a young girl: better to be a storyteller than an ordinary and overlooked face in the crowd.

Her father's example served her well. She used the very same tactics in describing her own accomplishments and life history. She mimicked her father's embellishments and his vivid verbal style. Later, she would also replicate her father's unorthodox methods of earning a living by performing daring stunts.

Hannah and Olé met and were married in Oslo. While living in Norway, Hannah gave birth to three children—Dora, Esther Nancy, and Olé Jr. They might have remained in Scandinavia, but on one of Olé's tanker voyages, he happened to land in Port Arthur on the Gulf Coast of Mexico. He found the area's economic opportunities appealing and decided to bring his family there.

First, though, he had to prove to American authorities that he could provide for his family. For three years, from

1905 to 1908, Olé lived in Texas, building a nest egg as a merchant seaman and cabinetmaker. Then, combining the money Olé had saved in America with earnings Hannah had saved in Norway, the couple was able to reunite. Hannah and the three children finally joined Olé in 1908 to build a new life in Texas. In Port Arthur, four more children were added to the brood—first the twins, Lillie and Louis, then Mildred Ella ("Babe"), and finally Arthur, whom everyone called Bubba.

It took some doing for the young couple to adjust to the way of life in Port Arthur. Norway had been cool and clean. Snow and long, dark winters had dominated life for most months of the year. By contrast, the Gulf Coast's hazy sunshine was relentless. Often oppressively humid and hot, Port Arthur's unpaved streets clattered with the sounds of horse and carriages, steam whistles from the docks, and clanging boxcars being unloaded by sweaty dockworkers. The air was usually filled with industrial fumes. Flames leapt high into the sky from refineries in the distance, and the mechanical sway of roadside oil drills was ever present. For these reasons among others, Hannah did not share Olé's enthusiasm for Port Arthur.

Perhaps to counter the gritty, polluted environment that surrounded them, Olé made a point of wearing a clean and pressed white shirt every day along with his overalls. When there were jobs available refinishing furniture, Olé returned to the craft of his father, fashioning beautiful items from wood with his slender fingers. His broad shoulders revealed his other job—eking out a living on ships that docked in Port Arthur's foul-smelling harbor.

Early on, Olé made a conscious decision to reject his cultural roots and rapidly assimilate "American ways." Unlike many Norwegian Americans, Olé displayed an American flag from his rooftop on every holiday. "I'm Norwegian," he liked to tell people, "but nobody's a prouder American than I am." Hannah preferred to savor traditional ways and share them with her children. Through food, songs, stories, and an occasional friendship with other Norwegians, she shared her heritage with her children. Babe tended to adopt her father's approach: downplaying her ethnicity in an attempt to belong to the new American society. This greatly contributed to Babe's own lack of identification with other Scandinavian Americans.

Mildred Ella was the family's baby until her younger brother, Bubba, was born. During the years before Bubba's birth, Hannah used to call Mildred Ella "Millie" or "Mine Babe." In Norwegian, *baden* meant "baby," so hers was an affectionate broken-English nickname for her daughter. As a youngster, Babe loved to brag that her nickname was derived from Babe Ruth, the legendary baseball slugger. Since she, too, walloped the baseball when at bat, she converted Hannah's term of endearment for her "baby" into the Herculean "Babe." She told this story so often that it stuck, even though it wasn't true. In later years, sportswriters helped embellish the legend attached to her nickname.

The growing family expressed their love for one another—indeed, all their emotions—frequently and effusively. This too was unlike most Norwegian Americans, who tended to be more reserved. However uncharacteristic, her family's emotionally open household meant that her parents, whom she once described as "sweetly strict," offered praise and love in greater proportion than discipline or criticism.

Babe's earliest memories bore witness to this harmony at home. "We all just loved Momma, and Poppa too," she said.

"We were forever hugging them and all that. I'd go lie in bed with Momma when I was little. She'd say 'Mine Babe, my best girl.'" As the children grew, the bond intensified. Thus, by the time Babe was an adult, her family was her anchor in a world where she was frequently misunderstood and not accepted. "Some families don't show their love for each other," Babe explained. "Ours always did. Momma and Poppa lived on for their kids, and they had that love from their kids all their lives."

Despite their isolation from Norwegian ways, the Didriksens did hold on to some important ethnic connections. Babe was quite proud when she was able to defeat other Scandinavians—Swedes or Danes—in athletic contests. There was a distinct rivalry between Scandinavians. Her favorite poem began, "Ten thousand Swedes ran through the weeds/pursued by one Norwegian." And at times the family celebrated cultural holidays. They were, like many other Norwegian immigrants, hard working, patient, honest, strong, stubborn, and frugal. They enjoyed smoking and drinking and did not always observe proper rules of etiquette, such as ladylike behavior or prohibitions against swearing or showing off.

Babe's childhood itself was an interesting mix of the distinctly American and the decidedly Norwegian. The house's interior, given Olé's woodworking skills and years at sea, resembled a ship with its fine craftsmanship and polished woods. It was crafted with items and know-how reminiscent of Norway.

Their languages also straddled the two worlds. Lillie, Babe's favorite sibling and Louis' twin, later recalled that all the children could speak Norwegian and "understood nearly everything our father and mother used to say in their native language." They fooled Hannah and Olé, who thought their Norwegian was incomprehensible to the children and who used it when they wanted privacy. Babe, Lillie, and the others delighted in their secret. In fact, both languages were used interchangeably in the home. Hannah, in particular, merged the two and her playful children teased her about it good-naturedly.

When Babe was only three, Port Arthur was devastated by a hurricane. The storm terrified Hannah, who worried over her family's safety. But it didn't bother young Millie (Babe), who scampered across the dust-blown yard as the wild winds hurled debris over her head. Her chore, assigned by Hannah, was to dive after the chickens that squawked and ran in every direction, buffeted about in the gale-force winds. A perfectly timed sprint and dive and she grabbed their scrawny legs in her determined little fingers. Clutching each one proudly to her chest, she secured them in the crate and headed out again in the whirling dust and tumbleweeds to grab another. Then she turned her determination toward grounding the large wooden washtubs rolling and clanking around the deeply rutted yard.

These tubs were precious to Hannah. To make extra money for the family, she "took the wash" of well-to-do Port Arthurites and returned their clothes clean, fresh, and smartly starched. The family needed the extra cash since Olé's employment was irregular. When working, he earned $200 a month—a hefty salary—but it was often followed by long months with no income.

Young Millie lashed those tubs down with clothesline cord and secured the knots as best she could. She careened through the screen door bringing twigs, dirt, and pebbles in with her—all propelled by the wind. She stood beaming at her parents with tousled hair, dirty knees, and scratches on her hands and face. As Olé and Hannah hugged her and listened to her breathless tales, they felt a mixture of pride and wonder. She delighted in their approval and thrived on the challenge of the unknown.

But the hurricane damaged the Didriksens' home, as well as Hannah's nerves. She insisted Olé move their family inland to escape the wrath of future storms. The family moved seventeen miles inland to Beaumont, Texas. In Beaumont, they bought their second house. It was in the south end on Doucette Street, in a run-down part of town near the Magnolia Oil refinery, the railroad tracks, and tanker cars. It was a grubby neighborhood with "a junkyard of odors pouring out of pipes and chimneys," as her 1975 biographers Johnson and Williamson described it. Long before air pollution regulations existed, towns like this frequently smelled rotten.

Over time, Olé built additions onto the house to accommodate his family, which now numbered nine. Each child had to contribute to the work of maintaining such a large household. The dust, oil residue, and clammy weather constantly left a film of gray-black soot that settled on the porch and on the clothes Hannah hung out to dry in the yard. Pride and well-taught habits compelled Hannah to enlist her family's help in waging a war against the never-ending filth. One of Babe's chores was scrubbing the porch that encircled the entire wooden-framed house. She would gladly let this and any other mundane task go unattended if there were any type of game taking place. But on occasion, she did her assigned job. To make it fun, she strapped brushes on her bare feet and "skated" back and forth across the floor until it was clean.

Olé Didrikson, Babe in front center, 1916–1917.

Beaumont in the years between 1910 and 1930 was a bustling port city of over 40,000 people. The town boasted that it was "the nation's greatest harbor" because of its freight stations, newly built wharves, railroad tracks, warehouses, and shipping centers. It was the hub of industries like oil refining, rice, and lumber. By 1929 the population swelled to 68,000 people. A full 25 percent of these were black; only 5 percent were foreign-born like the Didriksens. To provide for all the new residents, businesses like restaurants, hotels, schools, movie theaters, hospitals, and newspapers opened and flourished. The discovery of oil at the nearby Spindletop Field, first in January 1901 and then another gusher in 1926, meant there were even more opportunities for workers. Yet nearly all of the jobs were for men.

The choices were few for girls and women. Business owners believed it was more important to give jobs to men who had families to support. They ignored the fact that women also supported families. Many did not believe that young women were capable of being administrators, doctors, or newspaper reporters. The very few women who pursued those careers endured ridicule because people thought they were unfeminine. Women in all jobs were paid a fraction of what men earned. This situation existed across the United States, not only in Texas. That is why many women like Hannah resorted to running a business out of the home doing "women's work."

Because more jobs opened up for men, more families had some extra money for leisure-time fun. Beaumont became a haven for sports lovers. Swimming and "motoring" were favorite activities, as were hunting and fishing in the area's woods and lakes. Texas' warm weather meant sports were enjoyed year-round—a fact that inspired Babe's own desire to compete. The city was home to a Class A Texas League baseball team, the Exporters, who moved into their new park for the 1929 season.

Yet in the midst of all the hopefulness and liveliness that was Beaumont, there loomed an ever-present threat in the form of the Ku Klux Klan.

The Klan, a national group that had a particularly strong local chapter, believed in the racial superiority of white Protestant Christians. They terrorized blacks, Mexican Americans, and Catholic and Jewish immigrants. They also controlled Beaumont's elected politics and law enforcement agencies. Legally and illegally, the Klan imposed its own system of vigilante justice. They took one physician out of his home by force after he had been accused, but not tried in court, of performing an abortion. They covered him with scalding melted tar and feathers. This was done to intimidate and humiliate him—and to serve as a warning to anyone who dared defy the Klan's views. They insisted that immigrants and nonwhites were inferior and should be "kept in line" through physical and psychological violence.

The Klan reached the peak of its power in the 1920s. In 1922, when Babe was only eleven years old, Klan candidates swept Beaumont's votes. Many open rallies in support of the Klan were held. Clothed in their mysterious, frightening white robes and hoods, the Klan staged one mass meeting that year that drew 30,000 supporters to hear the Klan's founder speak. Shortly thereafter, 50,000 watched the Klansmen parade through the city's dusty streets.

The Klan kept its power by making their organization seem like a patriotic club that only wanted the best for America. But in reality, they lynched black, Catholic, and Jewish men, making these groups scapegoats for the nation's social problems. The murders were sometimes even advertised in advance in newspapers, and thousands would come to see an innocent man hanged or burned alive. Racism was widely accepted; no one was ever convicted for lynching a black man. The Klan swept the 1924 elections, and in 1926, 10,000 people attended a rally in Magnolia Park in support of Jefferson County Sheriff Tom Garner, who was a suspected Klan member. The Klan remained powerful locally through the late 1920s.

This is the atmosphere in which Babe's opinions about black and Jewish people were formed. The attitude toward "outsiders" was also why the Didriksens downplayed their ethnicity. To be openly different in any way could leave you open to ridicule or attack. As a youth, Babe internalized these hostile beliefs. So many people around her believed in the Klan's ways that she had no way of knowing they were wrong. In an elementary school class, a teacher accidentally misspelled her name "Didrikson." Babe did not correct her because the spelling seemed more American, and it always pleased Babe to do something contrary.

Thus Babe echoed the racist beliefs she heard around her. She uttered racist slurs to schoolmates and held unflattering opinions about Jews. Many other white immigrants throughout American history have made the same wrong-headed "choice." By seeing themselves as better than despised groups, they hoped to avoid hatred and ridicule. They also hoped to win the benefits offered by American society. If they appeared "normal," or white Protestant, then they were hired for the best jobs, were able to buy in the best stores, restaurants, and housing districts. In her later years, Babe struggled to "unlearn" these beliefs. Her experience is a powerful example of how the place and time in which we are born contributes to or impedes our tolerance for others.

Coming of age in this era, Babe had to fight to prevail in a tough neighborhood. She was dubbed "the worst kid on Doucette Street." Any window broken by a baseball was attributed to her. Any squabble over marbles lost unfairly in a backyard shooting match were blamed on her. Sister Lillie, always Babe's defender, said the blame was not always fair. Babe's cocky, boisterous personality and her skill in sports made her a natural target for blame. Yet she was developing into a rough-and-tumble adolescent. Olé Jr., her older brother, admired her, but she also intimidated him. "Boy," he later said, "that Babe was a cutter when she was a kid. I was much older than Babe, but she gave me lots of trouble. And she could hold her own." Olé Jr. recalled her ability to worm out of housework and her refusal to play dolls or house. "She was just too active to settle down and always wanted to be running, jumping, or throwing something."

Babe lived outside the spheres carved out for traditional boys and girls. Her parents, who loved her boundless energy and athleticism, encouraged her to compete against her brothers—or any boys, for that matter. Her father built a rustic gymnasium in their back yard that included a weight-lifting device. Fashioned out of broomstick handles, bricks, flatirons, and primitive pull-up iron bars, the equipment provided the children countless hours of fun. Babe knew "he put it there for the boys so they could strengthen their muscles. But . . . Lillie and I would get in there and work out with it too." Their parents, much more so than most Norwegian Americans, believed that competitive sports between girls and boys were acceptable. Few distinctions were drawn between what was appropriate for the girls and boys. As Bubba explained, "They encouraged us to be the best in everything we attempted to do. . . . We just did our own little thing, and whatever we wanted to participate in, we did."

Most female children in the 1930s did not have Babe's choices about how to behave. Girls were expected to hesitate to take risks, act less boldly, and give up more easily. They were told to be more dependable, awkward, dependent, obedient, easily confused, rational, careful, and nervous. If they enjoyed exercise and sports, then they were told to seek that in a male mate. For boys, acceptable behavior was far broader: self-confidence, courage, physical strength, endurance, self-discipline, cunning unscrupulousness, and competitiveness were all traits that boys were expected to have. Boys were also encouraged to have self-determination and ambition. It would have been quite unacceptable for a girl to think and behave this way in order to achieve her goals. As future mothers, girls were supposed to practice charity, patience, giving, and nurturing. Yet ambition and self-determination were precisely what guided Babe Didriksen as she pursued her dream of becoming the world's greatest athlete.

In all these ways, Babe's family and town greatly contributed to the direction her life took. As a member of a poor Southern white community, Babe was allowed to play outdoors unsupervised by adults, engage in rough physical games, use bawdy humor, and be a bit of a show-off. These behaviors, particularly by a girl, would have shocked middle-class society. The middle and upper classes valued moderation, self-restraint, modesty, and economic reliability. Poor people, whose lives offered little hope of self-improvement or self-expression, were more tolerant of "drinking, fighting, gambling, playing sports" and so on.

Babe internalized these male ideals into her own decision-making. The streetwise code worked for Babe on the dusty side-roads of Beaumont, Texas. Other poor girls, like Babe, also used their fists to protect themselves—even if it meant they were lonely and without friends. Cussing and smoking, too, were symbols of roughness and self-sufficiency and served as a warning to their peers to pay them respect. Babe, like some other girls in similar situations, behaved this way to show her courage.

Yet, as much as Babe was a product of this world, she was just not like most girls. Many of her peers still thought she was fierce and "boyish." In her Beaumont neighborhood, Babe's athletic ability was extreme for a girl, though not bizarre. Her behavior stemmed from her parents' approval, and from the ethnic interests, working-class ways of distinguishing oneself, and tolerance for tough women of her community. Even so, Babe was a unique creature: fiercer, more competitive, more atypical, and more self-reliant than anyone was prepared for. When, later, her talents took her beyond the confines of her own back yard, her "difference" was shocking to many.

THREE

"Not Nobody's Ordinary Girl"

It was an early morning in July, before the day's heat had reached its peak. Lillie and Babe sat on the lowest wooden porch step and turned the key to tighten their roller skates. The soles of their shoes were worn thin, but there was still enough of a lip for the clamp to catch. Babe stashed the key in her pocket and smacked Lillie on the back—the signal she was ready to take off. Despite the fact that most of the sidewalks were just hard-packed dirt, the sisters took the corner of Doucette Street like pros. The metal wheels of their skates whirled faster and faster beneath them.

They had a daily routine. After their chores were done, or in Babe's case avoided, they lashed on their skates. We were "all over the streets, always going from the house," Lillie recalled. They would check out the nearest dirt lot to see if any of the neighborhood boys were shooting marbles.

If they were, Lillie took a seat on the sidelines, while Babe joined in and bet her own cat's eyes or poppers on the match. Most days she left with more marbles than she came with. Lillie sat under a shade tree and waited patiently, even if Babe played for an hour. Sometimes Lillie perched over her sister's shoulder as Babe lined up her shot with one eye squinted closed. Lillie rarely spoke for fear of distracting Babe's concentration. But when Babe stood up, dusted off her britches, and waved to Lillie, she fell in behind like the good soldier she was.

On the next block were other boys who also went to Magnolia Elementary with Babe. They had rigged up a bar balanced above a sandpit and were jumping over it. As each boy cleared it, the bar was raised. Off came Babe's skates. Without waiting to be invited, Babe counted off the running steps she would take before she leaped over the bar. When the path was clear for her to go, she gritted her teeth and ran, pumping her arms as she flew. One, two, three, four, up! She cleared the bar easily, then landed hard on her tailbone in the pit. Determined not to let them see her in pain, Babe got up, sauntered away, and called over her shoulder, "Let's see y'all top that!"

The sisters were a study in contrasts. Babe was dark-haired, with an angular face and lithe physique. She was so lean her muscles rippled under her tan skin. Lillie, always referred to as "the feminine one" by schoolteachers and classmates, was blonde and unabashedly girlish. She was quite content to follow and applaud her sister.

One favorite activity for the girls was a game of "chicken," a contest that involved jumping from boxcars on a moving train that was headed for a tunnel. With Lillie at her heels, Babe would head for the railroad yard, an area declared off-limits by their mother. There Babe loved to challenge the local kids to match her, jump for jump. They would haul themselves into open boxcars as the train lumbered out of the station. The train's speed came close to twenty miles an hour as it approached the first tunnel entrance. Its deafening click-clack drowned out the cries of onlookers who cheered their buddies.

At the last possible second, the kids would leap off the boxcars. The winner was the one who stayed on the train the longest. It was a daring feat, because the faster the train went, the closer it got to the tunnel's front wall, and they had to avoid smashing into it. Amid shouts of "Jump!" and "Wait!" shrieks of excitement and anxiety filled the train yard.

With the train picking up speed, Babe hollered to Lillie to jump off, but the older sister froze with fear. Undeterred, Babe finally pushed her off. "Then she fell off too," Lillie later recalled. Shaken up, her knees and elbows skinned, Lillie was proud (and thankful) that "we never got hurt no worse than that." Other boys broke their arms, limped away on swollen ankles, and rubbed bruised shoulders. But not Babe.

Babe always won. She loved the performance and the danger.

Her mother had forbidden Babe to play on the trains. But Babe was not an easy child to discipline. Hannah was frustrated by Babe's repeated disobedience, yet she could not help being disarmed when her ten-year-old declared, "But I won, Momma!" as if that justified the game, the danger, or the results. Hannah's love for Babe was unwavering, despite her frustration at not being able to control her little hellion. When Babe got in really big trouble, Hanna would say, in her Norwegian accent, "I don't know where I got that 'ting,'" referring to her rambunctious daughter.

There was, however, predictability to Babe's misbehaving. Once Hannah made Babe a new dress that she promptly tore and soiled with grime at the playground. Angered, Hannah sprinted after her daughter when she saw the damage. But Hannah had recently sprained her ankle. Babe halted and said, "Momma, don't run. I'll wait for you." Hannah, who had been prepared to spank Babe, stopped short. Then Hannah looked at the girl and began to laugh helplessly, saying, "I can't whip you."

Sigrid Hill, a childhood pal of Babe's, was another willing participant in this naughtiness. Like the Didriksons, the Hills were Norwegian and had moved from Port Arthur to Beaumont. When Sigrid's mother died, Hannah Didrikson took Sigrid into her family. Babe and Sigrid shared a bed, as so many young girls in a large family had to do. Sigrid was frequently the one sent out to find Babe at some athletic field and bring her home. Many times it was a baseball diamond, where Babe was always the first player picked on every neighborhood team. Talking her into coming home was not an easy task, since Babe often convinced her to stall Hannah by explaining that she just couldn't leave right in the middle of the action. One more "at-bat" by Babe would win the game for sure. Both charmed and humbled by Babe's charisma, Sigrid loyally returned home with the familiar excuses. When Babe got home, her punishment was to be sent to her room without supper. She then asked Sigrid to raid the pantry for her. Sigrid tiptoed silently downstairs to get food for her bedmate.

Family members knew where to find Babe when she disappeared: Schoolyard, ball field, marble shoot—wherever a contest was happening. One such day was Lillie's graduation from grade school. Hannah sent Babe to the store ten blocks away to get ground beef. Headed home, meat in hand, Babe spotted a baseball game. When Babe failed to return, Sigrid was sent to bring home the missing youngster. Sigrid found her playing baseball behind the school with some of the best boy athletes in Beaumont. The grocery bag was on the ground.

Babe told her, "You take it and go home with it."

"You're gonna catch hell," Sigrid retorted.

Afraid to return without Babe, Sigrid too avoided going home. About an hour later, along came Hannah. The meat had already started to go bad in the sun. Much to Hannah's dismay, a dog was devouring the last of it. After Babe received her mother's angry words, she got "a good lickin.'"

The incident was a turning point in Babe's relationship with her mother. "Poor Momma!" Babe said to herself. "I felt real bad about the way I'd let her down on a night when she had so much to do," she said years later. From then on, Babe resolved to ease Hannah's life, not complicate it. She kept this promise throughout her adult life.

Lillie and Hannah never tired of telling stories about Babe. One of Lillie's favorites occurred in 1925, when Babe was fourteen. Christine McCandless, a neighbor, performed with the Ringling Brothers circus troupe. Lillie and Babe, after much pleading, were allowed to join McCandless in California, while she trained for the upcoming season of performances. Lillie recalled that Momma "thought Babe might turn into a good trapeze artist from things she had seen Babe do around the place when playing." In this supportive environment, the sisters had a terrific time, while "Babe learned to hang by her toes, turn flips in the air, and walk the tight-rope without the umbrella." Hannah sent for them at Christmas to come home. Considering her prowess, it is unclear why Babe never pursued the circus life. Her only souvenir of the adventure was a photo of Babe, Christine, and Lillie riding "The Biggest Elephant in the World."

The adolescent Babe received a good deal of attention, not just from family members, neighbors, and classmates, but from teachers and principals as well. Most everything about her was unusual, most notably her ruffian behavior and her personality. Those close to her found her charismatic, but also alienating. Many who knew her as a youngster remembered her loyalty, her disarming appeal, and her humor. But she also teased others—unkindly at times—and grew so self-confident that she could be a braggart.

At Magnolia Elementary School, Babe stood out for her pranks as much as for her versatility in sports. She won the marble championship against much older classmates. In baseball Babe was better than any of the kids in her class. But neither of those was the most memorable event recalled by her school principal, Effie Piland. "One day I heard the kids yelling for me," she said. "I went outside and there was Mildred, sitting on top of the flagpole." Babe had shinnied all the way to the top and stayed there until the principal demanded that she come down.

Reagan Baker, the constable of Jefferson County, Texas, knew Babe from their childhood. His family owned an icehouse. Back then, refrigerators were too costly except for well-to-do families, and folks used iceboxes instead. These were freestanding, metal-lined, wooden cabinets that held the food along with a block of ice to keep it cool. A drip pan beneath caught the water melting from the ice. Since ice needed to be replenished every day, the ice truck was a familiar sight. Like all kids trying to escape the summer's heat, Babe would ask the deliveryman for small chips to suck on. But, Reagan said, "If we didn't let her have it, she sure would turn loose on us." "Yup," he concluded, "that was the baddest little young'un!"

As Babe moved on to David Crockett Junior High, she became even more competitive with boys and less interested in girls' games and, for that matter, their friendships. "As far back as I can remember I played with boys rather than girls," she told a newspaper reporter some years later. "The girls did not play games that interested me. I preferred baseball, football, foot racing, and jumping with the boys, to hopscotch and jacks and dolls, which were about the only things girls did. I guess the habit of playing with boys made me too rough for the girls' games. Anyway, I found them too tame."

While Babe was one of the best-liked athletes in junior high school, some students avoided her because they disliked her attitude. A female classmate remembered, "One time Babe came down the hall where I was, and just by the way of a friendly greeting, she slapped me on the shoulder. Her 'gentle' slap nearly floored me and sent me staggering half the length of the hall." Two teammates also recalled Babe's traits of fun and roughness. "We all liked Babe. She was so good-humored," Edwina Lockhart said. "We were afraid of her, though. She would go around hitting us on the arms with her knuckles to make our muscles knot up."

Babe behaved aggressively for a number of reasons. She often assumed the role of protector for Lillie and even for her brothers. They appreciated her staunch defense of them, verbally and physically. If neighborhood kids became too rough or made cruel comments, Babe intervened, and her

brothers and sister admired her bravery. But Babe was sub-
jected to unkind remarks about her boyish appearance and
rough ways. Perhaps she decided that if she could not be
understood, at least she would be respected, even feared.
Finally, Babe's childhood neighborhood was itself a tough
place. Children roamed out of doors for hours every day
without parental supervision. Might ruled. The child with
the strongest personality and most intimidating power
decided which game would be played, how teams would be
chosen, and how disputes would be settled. Babe claimed the
position usually held by an aggressive boy. Her intensity and
fierce physicality served her well in sports, but it repeatedly
caused problems in more casual settings.

Once, as an adult in a restaurant, a drunk patron taunted Babe about her athletic records. He said any schoolboy
could have beaten her. She tried to ignore him. But as his
prodding nastiness escalated, she grabbed him by the shirt
collar and flung him to the floor. She was instantly humili-
ated by what she had done and regretted deeply that she had
been provoked to that response. Aware of the need to serve
as a role model for children, she rarely spoke of this event.
She became even more determined to find acceptable means
of settling disputes and expressing feelings.

She was at her best when she focused her energies on athletic quests. Even as a young teenager, Babe knew exactly
what she wanted to be when she grew up. When she was
small, her father Olé read newspaper coverage of Olympic
athletes to Babe, and she was enthralled with their abilities.
In 1928, as the whole family listened to the results of the
Olympics on the radio, seventeen-year-old Babe declared,
"My goal is to be the greatest athlete that ever lived." She
was determined to be an Olympian. Without coaches,

training programs, or top-level competition to assist her, Babe chased a dream that might have discouraged someone else. What she did have was raw talent—and plenty of it.

Her sidekick Lillie shared her Olympic hopes. Despite the differences in their abilities, Babe announced that Lillie would be a runner and she herself a hurdler and jumper. They practiced endlessly. To train herself, Babe hurdled over the seven hedges of the Doucette Street yards between their house and the corner grocery. One hedge was higher than the rest and fouled up her rhythm. "I couldn't get over it," she said. "That sort of messed up my practicing."

Babe liked to tell the "story" of how she politely approached this neighbor and asked him to trim his hedge and how he graciously complied. In fact, she was completely brassy about the matter. True, she first approached each neighbor and asked if they wouldn't mind snipping the hedges, which were taller than she was. The first request was courteous, yet bold for a young teen. All but one neighbor complied. However, when she was faced with one hedge that was still too high, Babe returned to the holdover's doorstep and rapped loudly on the screen. When he appeared, the determined young woman, hands on hips, declared, "I'm Babe Didrikson. I thought I asked you three days ago to cut those hedges!" Cornered, the recalcitrant yard owner grabbed his shears and did the trimming right then and there, as Babe looked on approvingly.

With the hedges now uniform, the sisters raced down Doucette. To avoid the broad scratchy surface of the foliage, Babe developed an unusual hurdling style. As she leapt into the air, her right leg splayed out straight in front of her. But instead of extending her left leg behind her, which was the conventional style, she crooked her left knee to lift her left shin up and away from the bushes. She kept this unorthodox style throughout her track career, even though some advisors pressured her to straighten out her left leg.

Lillie raced alongside the hurdling Babe, always preferring the flat pavement. At these moments, Babe and Lillie were soulmates, linked through their concentration and their desire to win. They were racing against each other, and despite the obvious burden of hurdling, Babe tried mightily to beat Lillie to the finish. "I didn't beat her very often, though," she later said; because Lillie "had too much fight in her to want to lose." High praise, indeed, when given by the toughest competitor of them all.

Lillie, clearly, was also becoming a competitor. But for Babe, winning was what mattered. It was always at the center of her spirit. The rest—good sportsmanship, fair play, kind words to teammates and recognition of her own physical limits—would have to be learned and understood.

FOUR

Searching for Belonging:
On and Off the Field

Babe's teenage years at Beaumont High School were bittersweet. As an athlete, she was a respected leader and record-setter. As a young woman, she was a mystery to many, an outcast to some, inexplicable to others.

Photos from that time show Babe, according to one biographer, as a "squinty, pugnacious kid with straight hair and severe bangs, dressed in a formless cotton frock, sagging socks, and flat shoes. She never wore jewelry, abhorred makeup, and didn't own a pair of silk stockings or a girdle." She was drastically different from the fashionable girls, with their curled hair, flirtatious mannerisms, and well-fitting stylish blouses and skirts. These girls came from middle-class families—their fathers were businessmen and professionals whose incomes had swelled during Beaumont's prosperous decades—and their looks reflected middle-class ideals as well as manners. Babe had more in common with the other working-class girls, particularly her teammates. Yet even next to them, Babe was by far the plainest dresser as well as the most muscular.

Her classmates viewed Babe as a friendly girl and a practical joker. But she was rowdy. Most girls in her high school were concerned with dating and joining the most popular cliques, such as Beaumont High's Kackler Klub. Babe avoided their companionship and shunned their desire for romance and socializing with boys. The boys in her school saw Babe as a ruffian. They rebuffed her, unless they were also members of one of the sports teams she joined.

Babe was the ultimate tomboy. Many at school considered her boyishness endearing. After puberty, her foray into male territory would typically have been over; instead, Babe's unfeminine behavior persisted long after the culturally acceptable age.

As Babe grew older, she became a curiosity. Unlike Babe, Lillie abandoned her racing and tree-climbing to pursue more ladylike activities: dating boys, helping her mother at home, and adopting a quiet, self-effacing temperament. On the other hand, Babe, for many years, resisted the pressures to conform to others' expectations.

In Sigrid Hill's opinion, "Lots of people thought she was a boy. She was tough." Sigrid realized Babe fit neither category.

For instance, Babe met verbal or physical challenges and taunts head-on, as a tough boy would. On one occasion, "Red" Reynolds, halfback on the Royal Purple football team, challenged her to box against him in a boys' gym class. "Hit me as hard as you can," he taunted. "You can't hurt me."

Babe took one look at him and threw a punch. "The next thing I knew," Reynolds admitted, "I was lying on the gym floor and they were pouring water on me to clear the bells and birdies out of my head. That gal really gave me the K.O."

At times Babe took her fisticuffs to the streets. One morning Babe turned up at school with her knuckles skinned. Her basketball teammates asked her what was wrong. "Oh, I passed a bunch of Negro kids on my way to school and one of them cussed me," she replied. "I had to clean up the whole gang."

Another classmate later suggested that Babe wasn't really tough, "just sure of herself." Because she was so athletic, she knew she could do everything in athletics well "and wasn't bashful about telling you about it." Even teachers occasionally were at the receiving end of Babe's sharp remarks. Never in awe of school authorities, she frequently pulled pranks that tested their patience. As a classmate remembered, Babe one day "scampered up the rafters high above the gymnasium floor" while it was being decorated for a carnival. She had to be threatened before she came down. Mrs. Whitaker, her former cooking teacher, recoiled with the memory of the day a large rat appeared in Babe's classroom. She herded the rodent into a corner and announced she had trapped it in a box. When the rest of the class returned to their places, Babe coaxed the rat out of the corner. Everyone panicked all over again. No one was amused by this stunt except Babe, who thought it was a hoot. The cooking instructor warned Babe repeatedly not to call her "little sugar" in or out of class. Babe grinned at her and said, "All right, little sugar, I won't call you that."

Despite her uncouth ways, Beaumonters appreciated Babe's friendliness and humor. Mrs. Whitaker thought she was a loyal friend. Even after Babe became famous, she continued to visit "little sugar," who had been badly hurt in an auto accident. "Babe came to see me and wrote to me several times to see how I was getting along," said the neighbor. Thus the same young woman who threw punches also warmed hearts.

Obviously, Babe did not fit into any one category among her schoolmates. Because of this, she was often alone. Isolated from girls because of her athleticism and rough ways, she sought the companionship of boys. Yet her personal style overwhelmed the boys as much as the girls, so the boys responded by teasing her, even though they admired her athletic skills. At times she wound up without companions. Risking further rejection, she befriended other students who were outcasts, those snubbed the same way she was by the more popular school leaders. She protected those who didn't "fit" because she knew the pain of not belonging.

Neither did she fit in academically. Although she never failed a subject, her letters to friends were full of misspellings and grammatical errors. Math was difficult for her. Her former elementary and junior high school principal preferred to praise her personal charm rather than discuss her grades. Her deportment, he said, was "outstanding. I remember her, as I'm sure do all of her teachers, as being very congenial and cooperative."

Sports competitions were where she shone. Her talent in diverse sports dazzled the whole community. Basketball, tennis, golf—whatever game she tried, she was a natural.

During her years at Beaumont High, Babe competed on the golf, tennis, and basketball teams. In later years, she claimed she had never played these sports before. She went so far as to say she had not picked up a golf club until after the 1932 Olympics. But a schoolmate who caddied for Babe at the nine-hole municipal golf course remembered, "Nobody had to teach Babe how to hit a golf ball. She had great confidence. She believed she could do anything—and she could."

Tennis? A photo in the school's yearbook, the *Pine Burr* of 1929, showed her, hands clasped behind her back and wearing a loose-fitting white dress, looking coolly confident among the tennis team's seven members. Babe and Lois Blanchette easily won the school's doubles crown, which qualified them for the state meet.

Basketball? Babe's physical education teacher, Beatrice Lytle, proudly declared she "started Babe on her basketball career and taught her shooting style, fitness, and fundamentals." The 1928 Royal Purple team photo shows twelve shorthaired teenagers in baggy V-necked tops with their team's insignia emblazoned. In the front row stands Babe, hands once again behind her back, squinting a smile.

That was the year female athletes were liberated from bloomers. Previously, girls on the basketball team, in keeping with the period's notions of modesty, were forced to wear ankle-length pantaloons under knee-length jumpers. Most female athletes hated them: They were heavy, woolen, scratchy, and cumbersome. Babe was delighted when they switched to loose satin shorts. They caused a stir in the community. Folks were of mixed opinions about the decency of the "skimpy" outfits. But all the girls were relieved to have more freedom of movement.

Babe led the basketball team to championships in two consecutive years. She was aggressive on court, using her body to bump opponents on offense. When she charged toward the basket for a lay-up, she would send defenders crashing to the floor. She was a smooth outside shooter as well; her perimeter shots seemed to float through the net.

The local newspaper, the *Beaumont Journal,* covered both the girls' and the boys' teams. Babe was frequently featured for her point totals, strong defense, and tireless energy. In her junior year she was the team's highest scorer. A local writer, "Tiny" Bill Scurlock, adored Babe's skill and style. He wrote about her in glowing terms and encouraged Beaumonters to get out to the gym to watch this terrific ball player.

Nor was her ability limited to the traditional girls' sports. Football Coach Dimmitt tried to recruit her to be a place kicker for the boys' football team, an idea unheard of in the 1920s. High school authorities nixed the plan, but it planted the seed of a future stunt in Babe's mind, one that she would carry out years later.

Nevertheless, Babe's athletic abilities made her unacceptable to the more conventional, socially elite girls in school. They rejected Babe and she rejected them. The tension between them made simple daily tasks awkward. Whether walking down the corridor or getting books out of her locker, Babe was stared at. Girls whispered secrets about her behind their hands. Yet the same youngsters would call out, "Great game, Babe!" and "We know you can whip 'em this weekend." She was both a hero and an outcast. One response built confidence, the other tore it down.

Her classmates were not alone in their mixed reaction to her. Reporters' description of Babe in her late teens showed confusion, condemnation, and, oddly, admiration. One reporter wrote that she was a "thin, muscular girl with a body like a Texas cowpuncher, an unfeminine looking, hard-bitten creature." He assured his readers that she was not "a freakish looking character," but a "normal, healthy, boyish-looking girl." He did note an undeniable "strangeness and mystery" about her that fascinated her ever-growing public. Others found her muscular build appalling.

Babe knew she was constantly being judged by people who did not know her personally, but saw her only when she competed in a sport or was interviewed. One reporter noted that, mindful of this scrutiny, she went out of her way to be a crowd-pleaser and a friendly woman. Indeed, by her mid-teens, Babe began to understand the power the press held to portray her favorably or not. So she went out of her way to be communicative and funny. She was always available for a tart comment. Gradually, she learned that in this way, she could control at least some of what was written about her.

The issue of her femininity—or lack of it—continued well beyond high school. The truth was that she did, at times, excel in traditional female pursuits. In homemaking Babe remained competitive. Her sewing skills were frequently cited. Babe won first place in the South Texas State Fair for a dress she had stitched in her home economics class. Years later, Babe embellished the story, saying she had won the prize at the far larger Texas State Fair.

But Babe's patience with her sewing projects had limits, as her high school home economics teacher recalled. "Babe made a little blue dress with long sleeves, and after she finished it and got a grade on it, she whacked the sleeves off nearly to the shoulder because they got in her way."

She never dated. Years later, in her autobiography, she created stories that portrayed her as popular and dating boys. The stories were fiction, but they revealed how painfully aware she was that she was anything but a typical teenaged girl.

The only places she truly felt she belonged were in competitive sports and with her loving family. Babe's intense love for her parents inspired her to succeed. Her family sheltered her from controversy.

Hannah and Olé were poor, but pride and self-determination kept them from accepting charity. A childhood friend of Babe's, Raymond Alford recalled, "We went barefoot all the time. Some of us never did have shoes. Everyone was poor." Babe wore shoes rarely—to school and Sunday church—the rest of the time she was barefoot to save shoe leather. She probably preferred it too!

Babe's gratitude to her parents helped motivate her to win. She understood that if she achieved enough from her athletic skills, she might be able to earn enough to help her family escape poverty. "There were times when things were plenty tough," she acknowledged. "For several years there, Poppa couldn't get work regularly. He had to go back to sea now and again when he couldn't find any jobs in Beaumont." Memories of her beloved mother hunched over the washtub scrubbing the clean clothes of well-to-do Beaumonters haunted Babe. "All of us pitched in and helped her, so she wouldn't wear herself out. Little as I was, I'd wear my knuckles down scrubbing on that wash board." As Babe and Lillie hauled home the wagon loaded with sixteen or seventeen dollars' worth of one week's groceries for the family, Babe became aware of the money needed to feed, clothe, and shelter her parents and siblings. To make do on what little they had, "Momma had to go in for things like soup that were inexpensive, but filling and nourishing."

Along with fierce pride and self-determination, mutual responsibility was a trait she carried with her into adulthood. Belonging to the Didrikson clan meant that you shared everything. Babe contributed to the family's lean finances even as a very young girl. She earned 10¢ for brushing Sigrid's mother's hair. This was an honorable way, all agreed, for Babe to "earn" a dime. At age twelve, her first after-school job was at the local fig plant. This paid her 30¢ an hour. Babe had to find the bad spots on the figs, peel them off, clean them, and toss them back in the trough. Many an hour Babe's young hands burned from the acid in the figs. The plant owners advised workers to wear gloves to protect their skin, but Babe could not afford to buy them. As her hands waded through the slimy fruit, she could imagine Hannah similarly hunched over her wash tub. She saw other poor neighborhood mothers trudging slowly up Doucette Street after a long day of cleaning rich ladies' houses. Everywhere Babe looked, women worked so hard that they looked old by the age of thirty. And they never seemed to get ahead.

Babe's sore hands made it nearly impossible for her to grip a baseball. No wonder then that she left the fig plant and took a better-paying job at the nearby potato gunnysack factory. She was paid a penny for each burlap bag she sewed together. This work was boring, the large needles dangerous, and the lighting in the workroom poor. She worked faster than any other employee. Her inspiration? She would slip out of work to play sports "and then I'd work overtime and everything to make up for it." These early jobs made her determined to escape such a grim life as an adult.

Babe kept only a nickel or dime of her wages for her own spending. The rest she deposited in Hannah's countertop sugar bowl. Babe urged Hannah to treat herself to something special, but Hannah always put the family's needs first. Through all these hardships, Babe learned how to be a survivor, to believe in herself, and to do what was necessary to care for herself and her family. With her family's love, warmth, and acceptance, she felt she could attempt whatever her talents brought her way.

As Babe's athletic talents blossomed, family, friends, local reporters, and Beaumonters felt the excitement mount. Babe loved their approval and pointed to it as one origin of her relentless ambition. As an adult she called this period, "Them hamburger days." They had little, struggled for everything, and Babe knew little peace. When opportunity came knocking, Babe was waiting at the door.

FIVE

Unprecedented Opportunities

Babe had a true friend and promoter in Bill "Tiny" Scurlock. His nickname was ironic because Tiny was a huge man who weighed more than 300 pounds. The lone sportswriter at the *Beaumont Journal*, he did all he could to keep Babe's name in print. He filled the paper's pages with flattering portraits of her as an individual and as an athlete. She was, he said, "flamboyant, down-to-earth, apparently gruff at times perhaps, but considerate, humorous, friendly, warm-hearted, and generous." When in her junior year Babe led the Royal Purple hoopsters in scoring, Tiny cranked up his coverage of her another notch by dubbing her "Mighty Mildred."

In the meantime, several hundred miles to the west, a basketball coach in Dallas, Texas, read about Babe's talents. In 1930, Melvin J. McCombs coached a women's semiprofessional basketball team, the Golden Cyclones, sponsored by Employer's Casualty Insurance Company. After reading Tiny's stories about the phenomenal Babe, he traveled to East Texas in early spring to watch her perform on court.

He was not disappointed.

After McCombs saw Babe lead her team to an exciting, action-packed victory, he offered her a position on the company team. This meant that Babe would have to take a job at the insurance firm. Employer's Casualty, like many other companies in cities throughout the South, sponsored an employee athletic program. Begun in 1924, the program was highly successful. Not only did the company get good advertising by placing its name on the team's shirts, but the athlete-employees turned out to be more efficient and reliable in their everyday work than the nonathletes.

McCombs offered Babe both a secretarial position and a place on the basketball team once she graduated Beaumont High in June 1930. Her high school teammates were thrilled about the offer, but Babe, still rough around the edges, handled the well-known coach's visit with her usual antics. Rather than listen attentively during a meeting with McCombs at the Rice Hotel, she entertained herself by spitting out the window, trying to see how many people she could hit as they strolled below on the sidewalk.

Nevertheless, Babe liked McCombs' plan and agreed to work for the Dallas-based insurance company. In fact, she wanted to begin right away. She would miss the last classes of the school year, but as she told McCombs, she needed to start earning money immediately. She would arrange to return to Beaumont in June to receive her diploma. (Years later, her principal remarked that while school records simply

Employer's Casualty Golden Cyclones basketball team, 1930–1931.

indicated she withdrew temporarily from high school on February 14, 1930, the records should be revised to read, "Left school to be the world's greatest athlete.")

Hannah and Olé were understandably hesitant to let their youngest daughter move across the state. Babe was hardly the kind of teenager who seemed ready for so much freedom. But Babe wanted to go to Dallas so badly that she talked of little else. She coaxed her parents into yielding to her plan to go to Dallas on the grounds that the monthly pay of $75—a great deal for a high schooler—could ease the Didriksons' financial burdens immensely. No doubt they gave in partly because there was a "team mother" and chaperone, Mrs. Henry Wood. Hannah, in particular, was comforted by the idea that Babe would be in the care of a mature woman.

Babe had already proven her basketball skills to McCombs. But that was not enough. She also set about dazzling him with tales of her secretarial abilities. She actually could type and take shorthand, but she bragged that she had won a gold medal in school for being the fastest typist. "I think it was eighty-six words a minute," she fibbed. She even told him that at the age of fourteen or fifteen, she had written her life story—in 42,000 words. The claim was preposterous, since it implied she could type more than one and one-third words per second and had written a 240-page book!

Babe jumped at the chance to go to Dallas because she knew it was unlikely that she would be able to make a living through sports alone, except perhaps if she became a physical education teacher. The combination of basketball and secretarial work seemed a perfect solution. Along with nursing and teaching, secretarial work was one of the few adequately paying occupations available to young women. Thus by accepting McCombs' proposal, she could play and at the same time soften her ruffian image.

Full of anticipation and perhaps a little fear of the unknown, Babe put on her prize-winning dress and took the long, hot, stuffy train ride to Dallas with her father. Babe had only a small bag of worn-out clothes in an old suitcase plus $3.49—the change from the money her new employer had given her to pay for the train ticket. It was the last time Babe's pockets would be so empty and her possessions so meager.

As a secretary, Babe was supposed to type and tabulate detailed statements of losses for the insurance company. At least, the company said that was what she did. The truth was that athletic recruits like Babe were rarely asked to do actual clerical work.

McCombs' recruiting policies were highly controversial, but not unusual. Women who oversaw girls' and women's sports nationally charged that McCombs hired young women for their athletic skills alone, encouraging some to quit high school, while discouraging the less skilled girls from playing. He was also criticized for doing away with demure bloomer outfits in favor of the "scandalous" uniforms of satin tank tops and comparatively skimpy shorts. In brief, McCombs and others were accused of creating an unhealthy environment that damaged young women's self-esteem and permitted the disgraceful display of the female body. McCombs, of course, denied all the charges.

Other semipro teams in the industrial league, such as those sponsored by Franklin Motor Car, Sunoco Oil, and Piggly Wiggly Groceries, were also criticized for exploiting girl athletes. The promoters of this highly competitive league certainly were not looking out for the best interests of their players. The teams were condemned by the Women's Division of the National Amateur Athletic Foundation, who denounced the companies' methods as exploitative.

Babe did not feel exploited. To her, this was a golden opportunity. Other female players were equally happy, since they could make almost twice as much money as their nonathletic working-class female counterparts. The best players, like Babe, were recruited from schools, recreational leagues, colleges, and Sunday school church leagues. Colleges in Texas, Oklahoma, and Arkansas also recruited female athletes, sometimes despite their poor academic records, with promises of tuition assistance, housing allowances, and financial aid. For young women like Babe, such an opportunity, coming in the first year of the Great Depression, was a godsend. As men and women all over the country were losing their jobs, she was beginning a career that paid more than some men's work.

Texans, for their part, loved to watch women play basketball in the industrial leagues that flourished throughout the 1920s and 1930s. From January through March each year, the sports pages of the Dallas newspapers were dominated by coverage of the forty-eight women's teams in the semiprofessionals and college ranks. Babe was relieved to find that the press coverage was not negative toward the women's strong muscles or competitive fire. What a relief after the years of taunting and sidelong glares that she had weathered! In this setting, female team stars were local heroes. Indeed, women's basketball remained the most popular spectator sport in Dallas until the 1950s.

Until 1930, the Sunoco Oil Company Oilers dominated the industrial league. But once Babe joined the Cyclones, the Employer's Casualty team ruled. For the next five years—boosted by Babe's performance, clever promotional events, and the presence of former major league baseball pitcher Danny Lynch, who was their coach, business manager, trainer, chaperone, and mascot—the mighty Cyclones were the most popular team in Texas. They routinely attracted 5,000 fans a game. Detractors denounced it as "the best team money could buy."

Maybe it was, but it was also a team that dressed for the part. McCombs, savvy about attracting the public to see women athletes' bodies, rejected prevailing conservative attitudes when he swapped the Cyclones' baggy woolen bloomers first for shorts and sleeveless blouses, and then even more daringly, for bright orange panties. Babe went one step farther: she had her uniforms tailored to hug her body. At the 1932 national track and field meet in Illinois, she shocked nearly everyone because she wore track pants, a sleeveless blouse, and no stockings.

The Cyclones won thirty-six tournament championships, averaging 38 points per game while stifling their opponents to a measly 11. Radio broadcasts (which began in 1920) helped widen their fame beyond the arenas, since fans that could not attend a game could tune in for a live play-by-play.

Babe's exploits quickly earned her All-American status in her first three seasons. (The first national All-American women's semipro basketball team had been selected in 1929, the year before Babe's arrival.) In the 1931 national tournament, she scored 106 points in five games and almost single-handedly led the Cyclones to capture the national championship. Reporter Tiny Scurlock, who continued to follow Babe, was so enthralled that he frequently inflated her scoring feats. He once wrote in 1930 that she scored 210 points in five games in Wichita and 195 points in six games in Dallas! Years later, he admitted in a magazine article that he had stretched the truth. "Some of the quotes you'll find are contradictory, but as you know, stories on the famous grow and grow with the years," he wrote. But Babe pumped up her record too, boasting that she had scored 100 points in a single game, even though it never happened.

In any case, it was an era in which sportswriters were much less concerned with accuracy than they are today. Writers wanted a good story, colorful anecdotes, human interest. Players wanted positive press coverage and praise. Thus each benefited from and advanced the other. Babe liked this arrangement. Her wisecracking was eminently quotable and she loved the attention she received. It was, it seemed, a perfect match.

During the basketball season, press coverage focused on

Babe much more than any of her equally hard-working teammates. Headlines such as "Beaumont Girl Plays Tonight in Cage Meet" and "Babe Didrikson Is Star of Cyclones Game" exemplified the special attention she received. A large caricature of her face, labeled "Mighty Mildred," pleased her immensely. But these accolades bothered her teammates, who felt slighted at her expense. If it weren't for those quick passes from them, she could not have scored so much. Some of them were fantastic shooters and great defensive players as well.

Her relationships with her teammates were strained, not just by lopsided press coverage but also by Babe's cocky attitude. She instinctively knew how to "psych out" cohorts and opponents alike. While this is not unusual now, seventy years ago it was unheard of among female athletes. When she first arrived in Dallas, Babe confronted the Cyclones' star basketball forward and told her that she intended to win her position away from her, which she did. Some of her teammates admired her despite her swaggering. Photos autographed by them were, in some cases, worshipful: "To Babe: The Best," "Love to My Speedy Running Mate," "Passionately Yours," and "To the Great God Babe." One sidekick dared to tease her, signing a photo "To My 'Low-Life' Girlfriend—Babe."

After returning home to Beaumont briefly for her high school graduation, Babe settled in Dallas for the long haul. In her new surroundings, hundreds of miles away from home without her parents watching and earning the monumental sum of $75 a month, Babe lived a life of relative wealth and freedom unprecedented among most women her age. True, she was watched over by Mrs. Wood, but the chaperone also had the unenviable task of controlling over a dozen teenage girls just like Babe, all of them experiencing autonomy for the first time.

Babe sent $45 of her monthly pay to Hannah, spent a mere $5 a month for a room, and bought virtually no new clothes. That left her the gigantic sum of an extra $25 a month for herself. The money not only lifted Babe's already ample self-confidence; it also clarified for her just how valuable her athletic skills were. What she believed she had to do now was "market" herself skillfully.

First, though, she had to distinguish herself in other sports. Besides basketball, Babe's "job" at the insurance company included playing on the company's other women's teams. Even among these stars, Babe soon shone the brightest. With unrelenting energy, she devoted herself to attaining higher and higher levels in each sport. Just as in high school, she was a handful for those supervising her. McCombs told the *Dallas Dispatch*, "Babe Didrikson was the easiest girl to coach and the hardest to handle of all the athletes I have had in the past fifteen years." She played practical jokes on everyone, alienated teammates with her cockiness, and was demanding.

At the end of the basketball season, Babe also played on the insurance company's softball team. A natural power hitter, she claimed she slugged "something like thirteen home runs in one double-header." Of course, she admitted, some of their opponents were lousy fielders, so routine outfield fly balls often turned into extra base hits. But her speed actually did accelerate many hits into homers.

In addition, Babe played doubles tennis and excelled in springboard and platform diving exhibitions. McCombs actually created a swim team with Babe as its centerpiece. He called it "Mildred Didrikson and Her Employer's

Casualty Girls." If he promoted her so brazenly, why shouldn't Babe tout herself as well? "I won diving events in swimming meets," she told reporters, "and I honestly think I could have qualified for the Olympic swimming team if I had concentrated on it."

Joining teammates who gave golf lessons at the Dallas Country Club, Babe was determined to master that game too. She practiced until her hands blistered and bled. She drove as many as 1,500 golf balls for nearly ten hours a day, trying to perfect her swing and distance. Lillie, who lived with Babe for mutual companionship off and on, was clearly disturbed by Babe's active disregard for her own welfare. "She'd hit and hit the balls," Lillie recalled, "until she had tape all over her hands." Come darkness, Lillie begged her to stop. "No," Babe replied, "I got to hit just a few more." Many a night the lights at the driving range silhouetted the young woman, all alone, slamming golf balls into the darkened sky. She stayed until she felt she had achieved a better swing or a few yards more distance. Exhausted—and only momentarily satisfied—she would trudge home, soak her pulpy palms, and sleep a few hours.

Despite all this activity, Babe was bored when basketball season was over. So Coach McCombs suggested she pursue track and field, and she agreed, in typical fashion, to try all the events, even though she was a little overwhelmed by the sheer size and strength of her teammates. They held eleven Southern track and field records and two world track records. "I'd never seen so many large girls—large feet and large hands," Babe recalled. "They were really husky."

McCombs taught her how to time her approach steps on the long jump, which involved dashing down a runway, leaping as far as she could, and then landing in a sand pit. He also showed her the mechanics of the high jump: running up to a raised bar, launching herself in the air above it, and then falling into a soft cushion of covered sawdust. And he helped her in hurdling: running across 80 meters of track and flying over each of eight hurdles positioned equidistantly. That's just about all the coaching she received.

On her own, she followed a relentless perfectionist's routine. She frequently pushed her body well past its comfort level. "I trained and trained and trained," she recalled. Her "second shift" began after dinner, when the other athletes were chatting, playing cards, or just taking it easy. Lacing on her sneakers, she ran throughout the Oak Cliff section of Dallas, where the team was housed. She kept at it until 9:30 at night. She would run down the hill on Haines Street toward the lake, then trot all the way back up. "I'd jog my legs real high and work my arms high to get them in shape," she said. Her arms were, in her words, "already about as hard as they could be," but she felt "they had to be better." Drenched with sweat, bitten by mosquitoes, shins throbbing from her hill climbing, Babe returned in the dark to her lodging. Yet even these grueling sessions frequently left her unsatisfied. She upbraided herself, telling her body that she should run harder, longer, more determinedly.

McCombs knew how she pushed herself, and it worried him. Her only fault, he once said, was that "she unconsciously and knowingly overtrains." He might have been sympathetic about her self-induced regimen, but in fact he pushed her just as hard as she pushed herself. During Babe's high jump training sessions, he set the crossbar at 5 feet 3 inches off the ground. At the time, this was the world's record. Whenever she cleared it, he bought her chocolate sodas. With that kind of reward, McCombs did little to help Babe learn how to pace herself.

At times she competed through a wall of pain. Just before a June track and field meet at Southern Methodist University's stadium, she stepped on a broken bottle in the locker room and sliced open the sole of her foot. A piece of glass lodged in the wound. Hiding the injury from her teammates, coach, competitors, and officials, she won first place in the high jump (5 feet 1½ inches) and set a United States record in the process. She also placed first in the shot put, the baseball throw, and the javelin. Her team won the meet, with Babe scoring more than a third of its points for these first-place finishes. Afterward, she wrote Tiny, "I went to the doctor two times and he gouged around," trying to get the glass out. The press, unaware of the foot injury, marveled at her wins. She was a young woman who made no excuses. You train, you work, you win. To Babe, it was that simple. In the letter to Tiny, she closed it with a postscript, "Oh yeah! Right after the track session I'm gonna train for the Olympics in 1932 on the broad jump."

Babe kept up on revealing correspondence with Scurlock while she was in Dallas. She consulted him about planning her athletic future, and Tiny also served as her link with her family. They sent her news through Tiny and she sent him clippings and warm greetings that he relayed back to them. She asked Tiny to be her manager; in exchange he promised to keep her name in Beaumont papers by serving as her informal press agent. He genuinely cared for her and the whole Didrikson family. Besides, he also hoped he would profit by representing Babe. They designed a contract that would have given him 25 percent of her earnings. He, in turn, would promote her and protect her amateur status, which was necessary to compete in AAU events. The trouble was that Tiny, although well intentioned, was naive about amateur sports' rules. He was gung-ho for her endorsing Fleischman's Yeast; while she pointed out to him that accepting money from Fleischman's would make her professional. In November 1931, Babe learned that it violated the amateur rules to have a manager, so she and Tiny adjusted their agreement. She had counted on him to protect her. But she quickly learned she had to watch out for her own interests as best she could.

Babe shared her hopes with Tiny—and her unabashed self-confidence. Just days after her first sweep at Southern Methodist University she wrote, "If I hadn't sat down on that last broad jump I could have broken the world's record just like taking candy from a baby." When she sent him press write-ups from other states, she couldn't help expressing her glee that she'd racked up more gold medals. "Just got back from Shreveport [Louisiana].... Well that makes the thirteenth gold medal that I've gotten. Made me a bracelet out of the first one I got and I got three from Southern Meet. All gold and no silver." (Silver was the award for second place.)

In her letters to Tiny, Babe's priorities were clear: winning and setting world records. After the Shreveport meet she wrote Tiny, "I am gonna enter the tennis, swimming, and every other kind of meets over here and over there, get full of medals. You know like ants."

Through Tiny, Babe sought ways to earn additional money that she could send home. So when another insurance firm invited her to play on their women's team, she was delighted. The proposal was for $80 per month ($5 more than Employer's Casualty paid her), plus medical care, access to a nonprofit cafeteria, and hefty bonuses—$25 per win in regular games, $50 in city tournament games, $100 in national tournament games, and so on. The deal never panned out because regulations forbade her from switching teams for a certain period of time. It did put ideas in her head though , and she would remember to ask for all of those fringe benefits in later years.

Her financial success gave Babe the chance to send gifts to her family. Still in her teens, she bought a radio on credit for her parents. (It cost almost a month's salary.) Then Hannah received a wicker bedroom set worth $80—another month's pay. Babe also bought Olé Sr. a new wardrobe and bought Hannah eight new dresses. As a surprise for Mother's Day, she had a new refrigerator and stove delivered to Hannah, who was so overwhelmed she cried.

Soon Babe began lavishing even bigger gifts on her parents. In 1933 Babe gave Olé Sr. a DeSoto automobile. This gift-giving put great pressure on her to earn even more. Some local Beaumonters criticized her family for accepting her never-ending gifts and articulating their ever-growing wish list. But for Babe, providing for her family made her wins "make sense and pay off." She once said, "Whenever I got extra money, one of the things it always meant to me was that now I'd be able to do more for Mother and Dad."

Because she put so much pressure on herself to help her family, she urged Tiny to force "a little more dough" out of McCombs and Employer's Casualty. Babe became angry; she was sure she was underpaid.

But Tiny refused because the ruse would have been unethical. It was shortly after this that Babe learned it was illegal for her to have a private manager, so she had to negotiate for herself—and she did it with the same aggressiveness with which she played sports. She hounded McCombs for a raise. He refused. In protest, she stopped playing basketball at her best level. McCombs fought back by benching her. Undeterred, Babe remained sure she was right. Her way of making a case for deserving higher pay may have been unsportsmanlike. But she was the best athlete, and she wanted to be paid for it. Male athletes received the fair going rate for their abilities, but not women. Babe felt she had to be assertive to be treated fairly.

While she was with Employer's Casualty, Babe emerged as the finest athlete in the United States. Her records and gold medals filled many pages: she was a two-time All-American basketball player; she won the 80-meter hurdles in 12 seconds at an AAU event (this record lasted eighteen years); she set an unofficial world record in the broad jump in 1931 with 18 feet 8½ inches; she set an AAU record in the broad jump of 17 feet 11¾ inches in 1931 (a record that lasted six years); she won the AAU softball throw championship in 1930 and set a world record of 296 feet in the same event in 1931; and she set the world record in the javelin with a throw of 133 feet 6 inches in 1930.

No wonder she thought she was worth more. Any man in her position would have been living in a mansion.

Still, a pattern was emerging. Her teammates resented her. Ever since Babe had arrived in Dallas, she had received special treatment. Sometimes she alone received free favors from the guy at the local soda fountain. "He'd say, 'How about another one, champ?'" They were infuriated when she bragged—and then delivered on her predictions. In front of her irate teammates, she fibbed, saying that the first time she picked up the javelin she "just reared back like one of those Texas steers" and broke the world record. Her teammates knew she had practiced relentlessly. Ironically, she was so intent on spinning a yarn that she fabricated a distance that was actually considerably less than her real toss. She also lied about her salary, inflating it to $90 a month.

Finally, McCombs made a peacemaking offer: Babe, he declared, would appear as a one-woman team at the 1932 AAU National Track and Field Championships in Evanston, Illinois. At least she could receive even more newspaper attention, if not money. Her teammates ostracized her, but that didn't stop her from going along with the plan. She comforted herself with harsh physical discipline, chatty letters to Tiny, her favorite snacks of strawberry sodas and onion sandwiches, and harmonica playing. She also kept meticulous track of her press clippings. They were sent to Tiny to hand-deliver to Hannah's "scrapbooks."

In 1932, as she began her quest at the AAU championships in Evanston, she predicted her one-woman team victory. And she delivered.

SIX

Olympic Gold

B abe was on top of the world! In Evanston, she collected six gold medals and secured a place on the U.S. Olympic women's track and field team that would compete in Los Angeles in 1932. After her victories she told reporters, "I told those other girls, 'Ah'm gonna lick you single-handed.' And I did!" To celebrate, she went out dancing with admirers and chaperone Mrs. Wood until 3 in the morning, although she still awoke early that day to work out.

The journalists, for better and worse, "adopted" her. Many openly marveled at her. A *Chicago Tribune* editorial raved that she "has started out to win the Olympic games single handedly.... Babe is hard to believe even when she proves it." Babe understood this was a turning point. She was ready for the spotlight. She told everyone—family, teammates, the press, and even passers-by on the street—

that she would win all her events in Los Angeles. She announced her plan to win all her events—and the *New York Times* delivered her announcement to its readers.

Babe joined the newly selected Olympians on the Los Angeles-bound train. She was immediately concerned that lack of exercise during the long trip might tighten up her muscles. So she propped open the doors on each end of the car, and, like lightning, sprinted through the train cars. She flexed and stretched continuously and on occasion leapt over teammates in the aisles. Other athletes chose to watch the scenery, play cards, and chat. Babe pulled pranks like swiping pillows from sleeping teammates' heads. She also strutted through the cars announcing her intentions to sweep all the gold medals.

In August, she told a Los Angeles reporter, "I came out here to beat everybody in sight and that's just what I'm going to do. Sure, I can do anything." She predicted she would set a world record in the high jump. "I don't know who my chief opponents are," she continued, "and anyway it wouldn't make a difference." Babe knew her opponents might read the papers; she was trying to "psych" them out.

A *New York Times* writer was fascinated by Babe's admission that she never played with dolls as a child. "When I was a little girl, I'd rather play with my dad's hammer or hatchet than fool with dolls," she declared, rejecting any "useless" girls' pastimes. The reporter made it the centerpiece of his story and wrote an entertaining piece about Babe's unusual qualities. Sent out over the Associated Press wire service, the article appeared in newspapers nationwide. It portrayed Babe as a "character," not quite female because she refused girls' companionship and games.

Some of her teammates were annoyed by Babe's antics,

and Evelyn Hall was one of them. In sweltering hot Albuquerque, New Mexico, the train paused. Albuquerque was rimmed by magnificent purple and blue mountain ranges and the air that day was wonderfully clear. It was perfect for a staged radio interview with the girl athletes as they disembarked. The plan was for each one to step up to the microphone, say her name, hometown, and which sport she would compete in. She could also say any other tidbit about herself she wanted to add. Many of the girls were excited, thinking this was an opportunity to send messages home to family and friends.

But the radio station's plan to have an orderly procession to and from the microphone quickly went awry as Babe took more than one minute. She borrowed a Western Union messenger's bicycle that was leaning against the sun-bleached train station and rode it back and forth in front of the stage, yelling loudly, "Did you ever hear of Babe Didrikson? If you haven't you will! You will!" Then she put the bike down and took a harmonica out of her back pocket. To the dismay and fury of her teammates at the microphone, she was cutting into their interviews with her loud serenade. This was a live broadcast and could not be edited.

Babe's Olympic visa, a type of identification card athletes were required to carry in the housing quarters, listed her age as nineteen. She was actually twenty-one, but had already begun misrepresenting herself as younger so that her accomplishments would seem grander. Her I.D. portrait was a study in determination. A tight stocking cap covered all her hair except her bangs. Her eyes were serious, cast upward, and she was not smiling. She looked tough and lean.

As they did the rest of the athletes, the inspiring opening ceremonies at the Olympics awed Babe. They were not terribly different from those staged today. A crowd of 105,000 filled the recently completed stadium. It was hot, and the spectators looked like a sea of white shirts and straw hats. Five thousand graceful doves were set free in the sky as the symbolic Olympic flame was lit. Amid this grandeur, 2,000 athletes from thirty-nine countries around the world filed into the arena behind their nations' flags, proudly wearing their special uniforms.

Inequality between men and women still held sway over the Olympic Games. There were very few sports in which women could participate. The American team had 357 men and only forty-three women. Among the eighty-five track and field athletes, few were women. However tough their competition might be, the women had a bigger enemy: the medical "experts." Experts in women's health, as well as decision makers for the International Olympic Committee (IOC), believed women and girls were too frail to compete in most sports. Physical educators, physicians, and Pierre de Coubertin, the IOC President, all agreed that terrible results would befall women athletes who competed in team sports. These experts warned that females could overtax their frail bodies or push themselves too hard psychologically. Too much exercise, they argued, would retard female sexual maturation, affect breast development, interrupt menstrual cycles, and make women totally unappealing to men. Worst of all, they cautioned that extreme exertion in sports could cause sterility in women. In short, they warned, the best female athletes were damaging themselves physically and psychologically, as well as ruining their chances to bear children. Because of these beliefs, Olympic rules limited women to competing in a total of three events.

These ideas sounded crazy to Babe. After all, she had just

won six gold medals qualifying for the games. Forced to choose, Babe decided on the javelin, the 80-meter hurdles, and the high jump.

At the opening ceremony, Babe filed onto the field of the gigantic stadium with the other athletes wearing a dress, stockings, and white shoes—all issued by the Olympic Committee. Although well aware of the brouhaha swirling around women athletes, her immediate concern was foot comfort. It was about the first time in her life she had worn a pair of stockings, and the shoes hurt her feet. So she led a little rebellion while the opening ceremony speeches droned on. She slipped off her shoes and elbowed the other American girls to do likewise. Their feet were pinched too and they gladly copied her.

Her teammates did not elect her their captain, an honor she very much wanted. She had alienated too many of them, and while the team's best athlete often was the choice, the vote was also based on getting along well with others. Babe had failed to build goodwill.

Still, Babe was determined to have the time of her life. She swiped Olympic banners from the outside of her dormitory building and led a mischievous brigade that took the decorative pennants as souvenirs.

While Babe was finding thrills in her surroundings, her ever-loyal brother, Bubba, was experiencing a grand adventure all his own. When a freight train slowed through Beaumont, he found a car with a door open and jumped inside with several of his boyhood chums. This was a popular way to travel for young people who had no money. Bubba had his parents' blessing to go watch Babe in Los Angeles on behalf of the family. He had $2.50 to finance his entire trip.

The slow freight train delayed the young men's arrival. The press learned of Bubba's journey to watch his sister compete, and reporters commented daily on his progress. The Didrikson family saga was good copy. They might not be able to afford to travel en masse to see Babe compete, but the brother whose battles Babe had fought inched his way across America to be there for her big day.

Bubba finally arrived at the fancy Ambassador Hotel with his grimy pack of buddies. Bubba took a seat "in those chairs where they had those doilies—and, well, my feet never did hit the chair before somebody had me and told me I couldn't wait in there." Thrown out, Bubba and the boys waited for Babe on the street corner. When she arrived an hour later, she could not have cared less that they were "unfit" for the swank hotel lobby. She was elated to see her brother.

When the two of them were alone, Babe slapped Bubba on the back and said, "Where the hell have you been? I've been looking for you for seven days." She then invited the gang back into the lobby. Now that she was there, the hotel did not ask the boys to leave. At the last minute, sisters Nancy and Dora were able to see Babe compete as well, although no one knows how they paid for their trips. Ironically, Lillie, Babe's favorite, missed seeing her sister in the Olympics.

Over the next three days, Bubba, Nancy, and Dora, along with thousands of spectators, watched Babe as she mesmerized the nation with her outstanding performances.

First was the javelin. The track's infield was so crowded with athletes, coaches, judges, and reporters that she stopped practicing for fear of hitting someone. When her first turn came, her hand slipped off the roped grip of the javelin and it failed to arch upward. Instead, "it went out there like a catcher's peg from home plate to second base," as she described it. However, this initial toss, 143 feet 4 inches, clinched the gold medal and set a new world and Olympic record. Unfortunately, in the throw she injured herself badly. The unusual grip and toss tore her right shoulder cartilage.

Just as she had done at the track meet when she sliced her foot open, Babe continued despite her pain. Her second and third throws were anemic, but she told no one about her problem. Physical weakness, or limits of any kind, were not something Babe tolerated in herself.

She approached her second event, the 80-meter hurdles, determined to prove her predictions true. She ran this race flawlessly, setting a new world and Olympic record of 11.7 seconds. Afterward, Babe told the press this was "the payoff in all the hedgehopping" she had practiced on Doucette Street in Beaumont.

Teammate Evelyn Hall was the second-place finisher in the 80-meter hurdles. Babe's gold-medal win over Hall was the first of the controversies to surround Babe. Ever the country girl, Babe said, "If it was horse racing, you'd say I won by a nose." But Hall saw it differently. She believed they crossed the finish line together, but that she actually broke the tape. She pointed to a welt on her neck to prove it. Teammates watching the close finish from a nearby tunnel signaled Hall with a hand gesture that she finished number one. Yet at that exact moment, Babe chided Hall, "Well, I won again!" With the words buzzing in her ears, Hall looked questioningly at her teammates and held up two fingers. Two judges saw the signal to her teammates. For thirty minutes the judges deliberated and finally declared Babe the winner. Nearly sixty years after the race, Evelyn said, "It's possible they made their judgment from this gesture of mine. I was heartbroken." Later in the day, a second photo-finish race led officials to reexamine the electric-eye camera snapshot of the Didrikson-Hall race. At that point, officials declared that Hall had at least tied. Had the first and second place finishers been from different countries, a protest could have been filed. But since both were Americans, the protest did not occur.

Hall remained bitter about her second-place finish. She noted astutely that "Babe had so much publicity, it was impossible to rule against her." History books simply say, "Didrikson, gold medal, 11.7 seconds, 80-meter hurdles." But for Hall and the other American women, who were annoyed with Babe's grandstanding and train-ride antics, it was a bitter pill to swallow.

Babe's third event, the high jump, was all that remained between her and a triple gold sweep. To add drama to the already tense event, she was up against Jean Shiley, her archrival in this event for years.

The two women tied with jumps of 5 feet 5¼ inches. However, Babe used a style called the Western Roll. Prior to the 1932 Olympics it had been an allowable technique. But in these games, judges ruled Babe's jump illegal because she dove headfirst over the bar instead of jumping feet first. Shiley was awarded the gold. Babe settled for the silver.

Babe left the field visibly angry. To Babe's teammates, her second-place high jump seemed the perfect justice for her grandstanding and controversial win over Hall.

Thus Babe's triple gold prophecy fell just short of reality. But she remained the center of attention. Her second-place

Babe practicing 80-meter hurdles with her "hedgehopping" extension.

medal for the high jump became the only one in Olympic history to be made half-gold and half-silver. It was a fitting symbol for her still-debated jump and for the mixed feelings about her.

Babe's Olympic experience highlighted two themes that came to dominate her adult life. The first was that for her opponents, a win over Babe held a special satisfaction, since Babe refused to understand that winning meant as much to them as it did to her. Her competitors wanted to dethrone Babe. This meant that every opponent would approach a contest against Babe at her highest emotional pitch. Babe's attempts to intimidate them sometimes had the opposite effect: they tried even harder to beat her. That makes Babe's wins all the more impressive.

The second theme the Olympic games highlighted was that in defeat Babe discovered she could transform a disappointment into an opportunity. Many sportswriters felt Babe had been robbed of the high jump gold. Among them was Grantland Rice, one of the most influential members of the sporting press of all time, whose prose raised athletes to superhuman status. Babe was flattered by the famous writer's attention, and he was smitten by her earthy charm. He told her he believed she had been given a raw deal. To boost her spirits, Rice invited her to play a round of golf with him. It was a consolation prize that led Babe to take seriously a sport in which she would eventually be regarded as one of the greatest players in history.

SEVEN

America's Newest Hero

It was a dizzying prospect, even for Babe, to see her name splashed across so many newspaper headlines as the undisputed superstar of the Tenth Olympiad in Los Angeles in 1932. There was no limit to the nicknames they gave her: the Amazing Amazon, Belting Babe, the Terrific Tomboy, Texas Tornado, Whatta Gal Didrikson, the World-Beating Girl Viking of Texas, and Iron Woman. The *New York Times* called her "America's Girl Star of the Olympics." Similarly, the *Metropolitan News Service* labeled her "the outstanding personality."

One reporter lamented that "when one looks over the athletic records of Miss Mildred Didrikson ... one cannot help regretting that there is no all-around event for women athletes similar to the decathlon and pentathlon for men." The decathlon was a race with ten track and field events, and in the pentathlon, men competed in five sports. In recognition of her astounding feats and her personality, members of the Associated Press voted her Female Athlete of the Year for 1932. It was the first of six times Babe would win this prestigious award.

Unlike some superstars, she was a pleasure to interview. Neither monosyllabic nor surly comments nor worn-out cliches for this athlete. The press flocked to her side because of her sports skills, but they stayed by her side because of her warmth, wit, and charm. Reporters were tired of telling drab stories of Olympic athletes doing their laundry in hotel room sinks.

Babe gave interesting little details of her life. When they asked Babe about her "beauty diet," she answered, "I eat anything I want except very greasy foods and gravy. I just pass the gravy. That's just hot grease anyway, with some flour and water in it." She said she loved onion sandwiches and strawberry sodas. These were tastes that young people during the Depression could relate to. Nothing about her was polished, predictable, or dull. Because she was so willing to share herself, the press gave her the chummy nickname, "Our Babe."

While the middle class who valued modesty, femininity, and playing by society's rules found her a dreadful role model, she quickly became a hero to the working class. Readers across America demanded to know more about her humble home life. They delighted to read about Bubba's train ride, how Hannah took in laundry, and that Babe stitched burlap sacks to add money to Hannah's sugar bowl. Endless stories chronicled her gifts sent home. She was praised by one and all as a caring daughter, generous caretaker, and loyal family member.

Babe was a pleasant diversion from the hunger and economic despair many Americans faced after the stock market
crash in 1929 brought on the Great Depression. Many
working people lost their jobs; banks failed because too
many people withdrew their money in a panic; and thousands of businesses went broke. Prices dropped so badly that
farmers could not earn enough selling their produce to make
a living. Many average folks, the core group of Babe's admirers, lost their homes because they could not keep up the
mortgage payments.

In such a gloomy time, Babe became a symbol of a self-
made American. She proved that someone could still be successful and achieve dreams even during the hard times. She
was, in some ways, a perfect American hero, one who had
seized the brass ring of success. What added to her appeal
was that she was not a spoiled prima donna. When one
reporter asked her about her "hand and eye" coordination,
Babe replied sassily, "That sure is a powerful lot of language
to use about a girl from Texas. I know I can run and I jump
and I can toss things. I just say to myself, 'Well, kid, here's
where you've got to win another.'"

Average Americans also appreciated her guts in taking
what was due her. Babe was proud to acknowledge when she
had hustled someone to even a score. After leaving the
Olympics, she disembarked a plane in Dallas carrying three
javelins. Why three? "Well, I got even with somebody. I took
one discus out there and somebody hooked [stole] it, so I
swung onto these three javelins. I come out ahead, don't you
all think?" she replied.

Texans hailed the Babe as their number one daughter. She
ideally represented the larger-than-life image Texans held of
themselves. Her success and unabashed pride exemplified

how Texans saw themselves as a people, a state, and a state of mind within America. Upon her return to Dallas, local papers hailed her as a "Wonder Girl." Employer's Casualty chartered Babe a private American Airways plane escorted by fifteen United States Army planes. Wearing blue sailor pants, a blue cap, and a dashing blue and white striped blouse, she was met by the thunderous cheers and applause of the Dallas crowd as she stepped off the plane. She posed on the top step with one of her three "swiped" javelins.

Camera flashbulbs twinkled like an army of fireflies. Babe drank up the attention. Her heart was pounding with excitement, while her hands nervously clasped the steel javelins. Her eyes could barely take it all in! Banners, posters, strangers chanting her name in unison. This hero's welcome exceeded even her wildest dreams.

The moment her feet touched the ground, radio station WFAA interviewed her. Then she was immediately ushered into the presence of high Dallas dignitaries. The mayor presented her with a scroll from the citizens of Dallas, "in grateful appreciation" of her "accomplishments at the Olympics." Next, a representative from the Dallas Advertising League gave her an award and joked, "Now that Babe has another Gold Medal, she's trying to find some place where she can hang it up."

Hannah, Olé Sr., and Lillie were there to greet her. "Mine Babe!" Hannah called as she held out her arms. Lillie, finally able to share in her best pal's excitement, wept with joy. All around them well-wishers beamed at them, applauded, and slapped the Didrikson clan on their backs.

Babe, her parents, and Lillie drove in the police chief's red limousine, which was draped in roses, in what Babe called a "monster parade" through the city's business section. Colorful confetti, tossed out of open windows by fans, wafted down upon them. Surrounded by all this acclaim, Babe's family members felt self-conscious about their disheveled appearance. They had endured a suffocatingly hot road trip from Beaumont to Dallas, stopping twice to repair flat tires. But Babe was not a fancy gal, and she thought they looked just fine. Following Babe's lead, the three Didriksons dropped their concern and relaxed in the regal limousine.

Lillie loved to tell of this wonderful day. "Big shots was all lookin' at us country folks, but we didn't care. Babe didn't care. We had our parade ride through Dallas—confetti fallin' on the cars and everythin'."

They went immediately from the parade to a luncheon in Babe's honor at the swank Adolphus Hotel. Speaker after speaker stood up and sang Babe's praises. When she finally got up to acknowledge all their accolades, she said simply, "I'm tickled to be back home."

That was it. She sat back down.

Hannah was beside herself with joy and pride. Babe grinned as her mother pocketed a linen napkin from her place setting as a souvenir. But when they emerged from the hotel, Hannah, an honest woman, regretted her deed and tried to return it. Thoughtful and understanding hotel employees insisted that she keep it. To Hannah, the napkin symbolized Babe's—and the family's—dream come true. She carried it home, washed and ironed it, and kept it folded up in a drawer until the day she died.

Three Texas towns—Dallas, Beaumont, and Port Arthur all claimed Babe as their own. Beaumont staged its own parade for her.

Beaumont's "conquering daughter" seemed completely

comfortable, perched on the raised seat of the fire chief's car. The whole city pitched in. The chief's car was adorned with a spread of roses made by the Women's Club. The Kiwanis Club, the Girl Reserves, Scouts, and Babe's high school teammates all participated in the planning and the parade itself.

Beaumonters also hosted a ritzy luncheon for Babe at the Edson Hotel. Her parents, as well as her brother Olé Jr. and his wife, were her proud tablemates. She received a symbolic key to the city and an engraved merit award from Beaumont's leading citizens. Her "Royal Purple" compadres from Beaumont High gave her an inscribed silver cup that read, "We knew her when."

Early believers in Babe, among them boys' football Coach Dimmitt and booster Tiny Scurlock, entertained the crowd with stories of her heroic wins. Dimmitt even told the hushed throng that Babe autographed 5,000 Olympic programs in one afternoon. No matter that this was physically impossible. It fit the image folks had of Babe and the story quickly became part of the folklore that surrounded her.

Tiny, Babe's ever-faithful supporter, had been the lynchpin behind the whole extravaganza. Several days afterward, Babe sent him a typed note on Employer's Casualty stationery. "Thanks, Tiny," she began, "for the party in Beaumont. I realize it took lots of your time and lots of hard work to put that over in the way it was handled, and I know you had much to do with that." Without skipping a beat, Babe ended her note obviously calculating how best to use the press coverage: "Don't forget to send me that scrapbook," she wrote.

While Babe reveled in newspaper accolades and parades, her Olympic teammates returned unceremoniously to their homes. Jean Shiley took the bus home to Philadelphia since she could not afford the more expensive train. Evelyn Hall drove back to Chicago, where creditors repossessed her car shortly after she returned. Participating in the Olympics took money, and unless an athlete was as aggressive as Babe, she could be left broke and jobless.

Before the dust began to settle from the celebrations, Babe struck quickly to capitalize on her fame. Very few Olympic champions had been able to parlay their gold medals into paying employment, but her instinct was to act immediately. Within one week of her wins, she got a court decree that allowed her to sign contracts and handle other legal matters. Tiny could not be her manager; that could ruin her amateur status, which she needed to compete in any sport. But now was her time to turn her fame into dollars. Babe felt the weight of responsibility to her parents, siblings, Beaumonters, Dallasites, and the nation. She had to act decisively.

The journey was to be far more complicated than she ever imagined.

EIGHT

Lessons Learned

Babe was determined not to fade from the spotlight. However, the years 1932 to 1938 taught her valuable and painful lessons about earning a living, surviving as a public figure, and becoming an acceptable role model for other young women athletes.

Tiny Scurlock knew how to generate coverage for the Babe even when she wasn't actively competing. He resurrected old stories that portrayed her as a remarkable athlete, daughter, neighbor, or simply an interesting character. At times he even made up stories to spice up the true tales. One extremely effective ploy was quoting Babe's predictions about her wins. The outcome of her predictions didn't matter; her bravado provided sufficient interest for his readers and her growing number of fans. He also once claimed, without proof, that she had won 634 athletic events. The second promoter that Babe modeled herself after was Employer's Casualty Coach McCombs. She had watched him recruit the best athletes, modify their uniforms to increase controversy and attendance, and advertise and promote his company's teams with precision and success.

From the combined business practices of Scurlock and McCombs, Babe learned how to "market" herself. For the fifteen months immediately following her Olympic victories, she began to put them to work for her. She began to understand the skills needed to be a successful self-promoter, and she became a self-sufficient businesswoman capable of caring for her ever-dependent large family.

But Babe was still naive about what would be expected of her as a public figure. The public had mixed feelings about her boyishness. She started to realize she would need to transform her appearance, behavior, and image before she could become an acceptable role model.

The press speculated that she was not a normal female. This was a constant source of tension for her. Writers portrayed her as an oddity, a not-quite-female creature. One story said, "She is not a freakish looking character . . . [but] a normal, healthy, boyish-looking girl." Another 1932 press piece said, "She likes to fight. Her voice is deep, her remarks virulent and pointed. She has few close girl friends and isn't much interested in boys." Babe was aware that portrayals like these made her seem peculiar and not a typical female. She challenged the public's ideas about how "normal" girls were supposed to behave. In a candid moment, she confided to one reporter, "I know I'm not pretty, but I do try to be graceful." Indeed, anyone who had seen her compete would agree she was as graceful as a gazelle in motion.

More frequently, however, Babe had little sensitivity

about the constant speculation about her femaleness. One reporter dared to ask her, "Do you—er—find that binding undergarments—er—what I mean is . . ." Babe, annoyed and possibly offended, interrupted him. "Are you trying to ask me if I wear girdles, brassieres, and the rest of that junk? The answer is no. What do you think I am, a sissy?" This kind of retort truly perplexed her followers. All young women were supposed to wear those undergarments, and "sissy" was a derogatory word that was used to insult effeminate men, not women. In fact, Babe knew she was female; she just did not like to be treated as a "weak" female.

Through her words and deeds, Babe created great distance between herself and other women athletes. In 1932 a reporter asked her if she was nervous before running a race. "Why should I be that way?" she snapped. "I'm only running against girls." For Babe, this meant she was better than "mere girls." Babe, like most Americans of her generation, measured women as second to men in power, strength, talent, and intelligence. Babe never wanted to be second in anything. Once again, her comment seemed to mean that she was not female—and that made her freakish. These early attempts at self-promotion gave outsiders ammunition to condemn her competitive athleticism and sexual identity.

She struggled to learn how to manipulate her press coverage so that she would not be portrayed negatively. Once again, Tiny Scurlock showed her the way. Having once dubbed her "a muscular gal with the litheness of a Texas cowpuncher," he now posed the rhetorical question, "Feminine?" and answered, "Decidedly so. She can cook, sew, and is a neat housekeeper when she stays around home long enough." Meanwhile, a *New York Times* reporter devoted three paragraphs to Babe's purchase of a floppy pink hat. Her sports victories were mentioned only in passing.

But Babe could not always control the stories about her. By fueling the tales herself, it created a painful series of labels and insults that hounded her for years to come. By nature, she was neither flirtatious, soft-spoken, nor willing to compromise. She was not self-effacing or concerned with an appearance that would make her desirable to men. Because these traits were part of who she was, she consciously decided to exploit her "difference."

She was not prepared for the viciousness with which some reporters wrote about her. The columnist Westbrook Pegler wrote an article in 1933 entitled "That Didrikson Babe Is a Sissy: And, According to Mr. Pegler, It Seems She Can Sew." He was trying to be funny in this piece, but he was actually hostile and ridiculed Babe. Taunting her accomplishment of the prize-winning dress, he asked sarcastically what she got for a prize—a flask? Suspenders? Shaving brush? Pegler even used violent images. The next time he would see her, he wrote, "I am going to walk up to Miss Didrikson and pop her right square on the nose. Then I am going to kick her a couple. Then I am going to chase her right out of town, publicly."

Other writers were even crueler. Some were very threatened and used violent language against her. Paul Gallico, a famous columnist, labeled her the epitome of "Muscle Molls" in a feature story for *Vanity Fair* magazine. He openly speculated whether she was a lesbian or even a member of a "third sex" that is neither male nor female. He implied that her athletic abilities were unattractive. Gallico said he was as curious about her as he was about "the bearded lady and the albino girl at the circus sideshow." He called her a boy over a dozen times. "Everybody in Los

Angeles was talking about the Babe," he wrote. "Was she all boy? Or had she any feminine traits?" He expressed pity, suggesting she was "not a very happy girl," because she was not pretty and "cannot compete with other girls in the very ancient and honored sport of man trapping." Later, he wrote a fictional story called "Honey" in *Vanity Fair*. Honey, modeled after Babe, was a member of an "intermediate sex." Gallico claimed she hated herself for her freakishness. Other columns such as "Mr., Miss, Mrs. or It?" openly discussed Babe as odd and debated which bathroom she should use, men's or women's, after an athletic competition.

Babe wasn't alone in receiving such criticism. A female sprinter, probably Stella Walsh, nicknamed the "Galloping Ace," was described by a reporter as "a big, lanky, flat-chested girl with as much sex appeal as grandmother's old sewing machine." For this writer, as well as the powerful president of the 1936 U.S. Olympic Committee, Avery Brundage, "beauty and success in girls' track and field sports don't go together well." All these naysayers were voicing strongly held cultural beliefs that there were two kinds of sports for women: manly sports and beautiful sports. Manly sports were running, jumping, throwing events, and competitive body-contact team sports like basketball. Women who played these were seen as rejecting submissiveness. Beautiful sports consisted of golf, ice-skating, swimming, diving, and archery. Beautiful sports were so named because women did not sweat when doing them. The participants wore cute outfits and unsmudged makeup or protected their hair with bathing caps. Sonja Henie, the Olympic gold-medallist ice skater in 1928, symbolized this acceptable female athlete. She used her athletic fame to launch a successful Hollywood film career.

Commentators believed the manly sports produced infertility and flat-chestedness. (It apparently never occurred to them that women who were naturally small-breasted could be gifted athletes or that so much exercise reduced body size and fat overall. Nor could they fathom that some people would find this physique attractive.) Articles along these lines appeared in *Time, Life, Vanity Fair,* and various sports magazines and newspapers. One doctor concluded in an article that among women "muscles, strength, strain, sweat, and dirt were offensive and unfeminine," and that musculature was particularly damaging to women's "real calling: motherhood."

As the finest female athlete of her generation, Babe bore the brunt of this kind of prejudice. Dr. Belle Mead Holm, who later became Dean of Women's Physical Education at Lamar University in Beaumont, recalled how her gym teachers, succumbing to cultural pressure, "posted signs on the school bulletin boards reading: Don't Be a Muscle Moll." Her mother cried when Holm played softball, saying, "I just don't want you to grow up to be like Babe Didrikson."

Thus stranded, Babe was caught between pride in her athletic prowess and cultural stereotypes that ridiculed it. Little wonder that she kept her Olympic gold medals stuffed in a coffee can on her kitchen counter.

NINE

Stunts and Sideshows

Babe coped with her outsider status by becoming even more self-sufficient. She isolated herself from close friendships, comforting herself instead with visits with her family. Most important, she pursued endless roads toward economic success. To get attention, she recreated herself as a character—a quotable, even outrageous one.

Her newest tall stories made her sound like a female Paul Bunyan: invincible. She claimed she had had an injury-free childhood. Not true! Babe had all the usual childhood cuts and bruises, including the time she split her knee open while "skating" the porch clean in Beaumont. She claimed she had been offered an athletic scholarship to the University of Southern California to represent them in track and field. (She really had been offered a USC scholarship, but she declined it, fearful it would endanger her amateur status necessary for the Olympics.) She fibbed about her size, claiming she had only been 5 feet tall and 105 pounds during the Olympics. She also lied about golf, saying she had never played until the invitation came from Grantland Rice.

Actually, she nearly ruined her amateur standing in golf after the Olympics. Golf and tennis were the only paid sports then available for women. Yet all competitions that would prepare Babe for joining the pro ranks were conducted under the rules of the Amateur Athletic Union and demanded that she remain unpaid. So when an ad for a Dodge automobile appeared in 1933 in the *Chicago Daily Times* with her photo and a verbal endorsement, the AAU charged she had been paid to endorse the car and thus had violated its rules. In Babe's defense, the Dodge dealer and the advertising agency swore she had not been paid. Despite their support, she was barred from all AAU contests. She simultaneously resigned from Employer's Casualty teams in a daring stroke of self-assertion.

So now, a mere six months after her greatest glory, Babe was unemployed and incredibly frustrated. Were there ulterior motives for keeping her out of organized amateur sports? She thought so. After all, she was working class, loud, and aggressive. She was sure the people who ruled golf felt she would damage the sport's serene, demure image. She angrily declared she had been suspended because they didn't want her "to beat the rich dames." Some writers agreed that the suspension was, as she put it, a "bunch of hooey." Other athletes had accepted money for costs related to travel and had not been banned. The AAU's ruling seemed to single her out for punishment.

Rather than retreat into obscurity, Babe used this blow to gain sympathy. At a memorable press conference, she predicted she would do Hollywood film work, although no offers had been made. Then, as the flashbulbs popped, she announced she would swim entirely around Manhattan Island as practice. Then, the topper—she would swim the English Channel.

Babe now had the upper hand. The AAU officials voted to reinstate her only a few hours after she resigned, but it was too late. With encouragement from everyone around her, she was determined to pursue moneymaking opportunities, boosting her own confidence in the process.

In a daring move, she immediately signed a contract with Chrysler Motor Company to promote the exact car she had been accused by the AAU of selling! She even appeared at the Detroit Auto Show alongside the Dodge 6 and played her harmonica. Chrysler Corporation was delighted to have this premier personality in their corner. They introduced her to George T. Emerson, the representative of a major advertising agency, who arranged a contract for Babe to become a live, on-stage performer.

Her name was atop the marquee at the Palace Theater in Chicago in four-foot high letters, and she got the star's dressing room. The first day she arrived at the theater, she panicked briefly when she saw the customers lined up around the building waiting to buy tickets to see her. But she quickly recovered. She had never been a stage performer before, but she knew how to work a crowd.

Her grand entrance was all show business: she strolled down the aisle in a Panama hat and high-heeled shoes and launched into the song, "I'm Fit as a Fiddle and Ready for Love." Then she shed her feminine clothing to reveal her muscular body in a tight red, white, and blue jacket and satin silk shorts. It was exactly what the packed house wanted: a close look at the Amazon. For almost twenty minutes, she sang, played the harmonica ("When Irish Eyes Are Smiling," "Begin the Beguine," and "Jackass Blues"), and swapped jokes with her supporting cast. To demonstrate her athleticism, she ran on a stationary treadmill in front of a black velvet curtain while an ordinary woman ran on another treadmill beside her. A gigantic clock ticked off Babe's speed. Naturally, the other woman looked slow and ungraceful in comparison. At the end of this make-believe race, Babe surged ahead of her mock competitor and broke a finish-line tape.

These antics might have entertained the spectators, but they also demeaned Babe. At least the harmonica playing showed a real talent and avoided the feeling of a carnival sideshow. A critic from a local Chicago paper praised her, saying she "took the hurdle as gallantly as she ever did on the track" and "played the harmonica with no mean skill."

For Babe, being a ham came naturally. She was so good at it that audiences filled the theater four or five times daily to see her perform in Chicago, and she got advance bookings for shows in New York City. She probably earned between $500 and $1,000 for the week in Chicago, which was huge money at that time. The trouble was Babe hated being hemmed indoors. She complained to her sister Nancy, "I don't want the money if I have to make it this way." In yet another daring move, Babe canceled her next booking and walked away from show business, after just one wildly successful week.

In her hotel room, where she felt like a prisoner, she told Nancy, "I want to live my life outdoors. And I want to play golf." However, wanting to play golf did not mean she was ready to play, not at the professional level. She needed time to practice. That dream would have to wait. Instead, Babe pursued a series of stunt exhibitions designed to keep her name in the papers and "turn a buck." She set out to beat men at their own games.

She started by announcing in January 1933 that she would soon box against baseball slugger George Herman "Babe" Ruth. She tried to negotiate this on a trip to New York, home of Ruth's team, the Yankees. No deal was ever struck, but it didn't matter. Next she told reporters she hoped to meet Babe Ruth at McGovern's gym. "I never met the Babe," she explained, "but gee, I'd like to put the gloves on with him for a while. I hope they have a punching bag over there. Boy, how I can punch that bag!"

How perfect! The female Babe against Ruth, the male Babe. What a classic contest it could be. And boxing! That was a taboo sport for a woman. Accounts of her possible bout with Ruth ran in newspapers across America. It was a testament to Babe's skill at mythmaking that years later, some reporters actually wrote of this event as if it had happened.

During this period, Babe shocked listeners and readers with her ideas on womanhood. Once, kidding around, she convinced a reporter for a few minutes that she was married with two children. Another time, she flashed a diamond ring. "Bought it myself. It was a diamond I wanted, not a man," she drawled. Shortly thereafter, she retreated from these sassy remarks. "Of course I am going to marry," she snapped. She particularly disliked women reporters because they were most likely to ask her questions about marriage and children. Alternately a rebel or a conformist, depending on the circumstances, Babe was also reflecting her real ambivalence about herself. She was a woman pressured to be married and submissive on the one hand, and a hard-driving, aggressive athlete on the other.

Babe did line up exhibitions with athletes less famous than Babe Ruth. One was against Ruth McGinnis, a billiards professional. Babe claimed she won again and again over the years, but no eyewitness ever reported the match in the papers. (Tiny Scurlock bragged years later that Babe toured nationally shooting pool, another one of his fanciful fictions.)

Yet another stunt was as a guest basketball player on the Brooklyn Yankees against the Long Island Ducklings. Her team won, 19–16, and she was given a live duck with a ribbon around its neck as a prize. She kept it in her hotel bathtub for a couple of days until she shipped it home to her parents in Beaumont.

These exhibitions, however, generated little money. Babe and Nancy, who had recently come to live with her for companionship, were rapidly running out of the cash Babe had saved. And sitting idle was not Babe's style. The sisters packed up and went home to Beaumont. Babe hoped her remaining $1,800 would last three years, while she got tutoring from a local male golf pro. Alas, her savings were gone by the end of the summer. The Didrikson family had come to rely on Babe's large paychecks, and Babe owed payments to several companies from whom she had bought gifts on credit for family members.

Her need for both money and stimulating work was desperate. She returned to Employer's Casualty in Dallas to work as a paid publicist, not an athlete. She was extremely grateful for this steady income and she grew very loyal to ECC. She went back to them several times, and there was always a job for her at $300 a month.

In the fall of 1933, Babe's life hit bottom. She was speeding one day in her automobile when she accidentally struck and killed an elderly man. ECC managed to downplay this tragic event, paying the damages, hiring her lawyers, and extricating her from the mess. That fall, Babe's father fell ill. The family, flat broke, could not afford a doctor. They took Olé Sr. to a university charity hospital in Galveston, which was used for teaching medical students. While Olé recovered from respiratory surgery, Babe plotted how to earn more money.

Finally, she accepted a promoter's offer to tour American cities in a basketball team named "Babe Didrikson's All-Americans." Babe enjoyed this life on the road. The team competed against all-male teams only, a tactic guaranteed to get attention. They played in most major cities in the Midwest. Once, they competed against the all-male, all-black Harlem Globetrotters. This broke yet another cultural taboo: interracial sports competition. The All-Americans drew decent crowds. "We weren't world beaters," Babe said, but the team "had a pretty fair bunch of basketball players."

When the basketball season ended in the spring of 1934, the promoter booked Babe to tour with the House of David, an all-male baseball team that consisted of former big-league players who wore long beards that made them look like patriarchs from the Old Testament. Having Babe join them broke another taboo, since men and women rarely mixed in a team sport. With the addition of Babe, the House of David packed stadiums across the country and newspapers followed their progress with headlines such as "Famous Woman Athlete Pitches for Whisker Team."

Babe, at last, was earning between $1,000 and $1,500 a month, a large and steady salary in the middle of the Great Depression. One in four or five workers was unemployed. Women working in garment manufacturing in New York

City sweatshops earned only $2.39 a week. Economically, Babe was blessed indeed.

She worked awfully hard for the money. During the summer of 1934, she appeared in over 200 games from Fort Lauderdale, Florida, to Coeur d'Alene, Idaho. To maintain an image of propriety, she did not travel on the bus with her male teammates. Accompanied only by her maps and luggage, Babe drove herself to each ballpark. She would pitch the first couple of innings, get back in her car alone, and head for the next town or city. It was a lonely existence: one hour she was riding high, cheered by fans, and in the next she was drifting by herself on unfamiliar roads with only her car radio to cheer her.

Babe's pitching, while far above average, was hittable, so opposing teams agreed to "fix" games so that they wouldn't score against her. This was done occasionally in minor league baseball at the time. This brought more paying fans into the park and also stoked Babe's image as infallible. As a hitter, Babe was wonderful; no fix needed there. Once at Chicago's Logan Park, before 8,000 fans, Babe hit a long line drive, then ran the bases so fast that she stretched the hit into an inside-the-park home run. It was the only run scored by her team and gave them a hard-won victory.

Babe loved to dazzle spectators with dramatic plays. Grover Cleveland Alexander, her teammate and a former member of the major league Philadelphia Phillies, knew that Babe's performance largely depended on the crowd's size and enthusiasm. "With a crowd," he said, "Babe, she'd really put out, but if there was no crowd, she wasn't worth a damn. And the bigger the crowd, the bigger Babe's performance." She was as much an entertainer as she was an athlete in these games. Since the outcome was largely

Babe and the House of David touring baseball team, 1934.

rigged, she wasn't playing to win but to please the crowd.

Sometimes the stunts were downright buffoonery. For instance, one entire ball game was played on donkey-back by both sides. Half the struggle was getting the stubborn and confused animals to head in the right direction. As if this weren't ludicrous enough, Babe learned how to straddle the mule's rump, riding it while hanging off the rear end—true sideshow behavior.

One reporter said that Babe had "a physique that the average high school or college male would envy." So, to soften her image as a woman, Babe occasionally posed in provocatively feminine dresses, and those photos would appear right beside her mannish photos. In one series of pictures in the *Detroit Evening Times,* photos showed Babe in an evening gown, in boxing trunks hunched over and ready to jab, and in a floor-length dress with a purse and heels. At first, Babe had resisted putting on the frilly girls' clothes saying, "Aw, I don't want to get all dolled up like a sissy." But she finally agreed.

To supplement her barnstorming income and pitching exhibitions, Babe was filmed in short motion pictures that showed her participating in twelve sports. One segment was a series of staged football plays with the Texas Southern Methodist University men's football team. Babe wore the complete uniform: shoulder pads, tapered pants, and helmet. These sequences were carefully choreographed. (The films were staged by her sportswriting buddy, Grantland Rice.) As she cut back and forth across the field, her would-be tacklers kept diving—and missing. In one sequence she tackled one of the fellows. When Rice played the film footage at high speed, it looked as if Babe were outplaying the entire SMU football team.

Boxing was always a surefire stunt. She boxed the brother of middleweight champion Young Stribling, but as photos circulated, the story grew so that people thought she actually decked the titleholder, not his sibling. She even sparred with heavyweight champion Jack Dempsey. Then she pitched for $200 a game in the spring of 1934 for Cleveland against the New Orleans Pelicans. A few weeks later she pitched a couple of innings for the St. Louis Cardinals against the Boston Red Sox.

Crisscrossing the country throughout 1933 and 1934, splicing together exhibitions for $200 to $500 each, Babe grew exhausted. Finally, in September 1934 she wrote Scurlock that her golf lessons would begin the following month in Beaumont. In a postscript that surely impressed Tiny and the Didrikson clan, Babe reminded them she had vowed not to come home unless she had earned $10,000.

"Well," she announced, "I'm ready.... I'm really doing it."

Just in time too. Her promoters were urging her to race on foot against the horse that had won the Kentucky Derby. She almost agreed. Only discouragement from a few wise souls nixed the plan. While her stunts and sideshows had brought her good money and kept her name in the papers, they had failed miserably at the most important level: not a single stunt had been inspired by her competitive spirit. No wonder, then, she turned all her attention and dreams to golf. Golf alone offered her a future as a legitimate, respected, wage-earning athlete.

TEN

Eager to Be a
Proper Lady Golfer

Golf was the right sport for her now, Babe thought as she drove home to Beaumont. As a news report noted when tennis champion Helen Jacobs received the Female Athlete of the Year award in 1933, the "sphere of noteworthy feminine competition" was "relatively limited" to tennis, golf, and swimming." With golf, Babe could shed all the ugly talk and ridicule. She would be respectable. (Tennis might have worked in other circumstances. In fact, the physical nature of it appealed to her more than golf, but because she tore her shoulder ligaments in her Olympic javelin toss, she would never have enough power in her overhand serve.)

What had really fired up her ambitions to pursue golf was seeing the great golfer, Bobby Jones, put on an exhibition. While touring with the House of David, she had watched him perform in Houston. His strength, precision, and command of the game floored Babe. She even followed him to Dallas to watch him compete in tournament play.

Babe was not going to make a living through paid endorsements. Not a single female athlete endorsed a product in *Ladies' Home Journal* or *Vogue,* and *Harper's Bazaar,* which both men and women read, carried only one ad, featuring tennis champion Alice Marble endorsing sports apparel. The market was cornered by Hollywood film stars like Jean Harlow, Greta Garbo, Rosalind Russell, Rita Hayworth, and Barbara Stanwyck, who pitched everything from clothes to makeup to swimsuits.

Babe had to be accepted into the golf world first and worry about the money later. So she made a conscious choice to tone down her mannish ways. This, she hoped, would put the focus back on her sports skill. She had adapted before, learning how to give snappy interviews, turn a buck, and keep her name in print. If she had to be more ladylike to be thought the best and become the most famous golfer in the world, then that's what she would do.

Knowing that people loved to compare her skills with those of men, Babe calculated how much money she could make from exhibitions. She challenged male golf pros and celebrities to golf matches. She hoped they would provide the competitive inspiration she had so sorely lacked, and as a bonus, maybe she could get some tutoring along the way.

She made it hard for anyone to refuse her. If someone hesitated, Babe pulled out all the stops until they gave in. When Frank Craven, an actor and playwright, turned her down initially, Babe, never one to be upstaged, countered, "If that doesn't suit, we'll try boxing or wrestling."

"No, we won't," he shot back. "You've already broken my right hand just being introduced."

"Well then," Babe shot back, "I'll play dolls with you." Craven had no more excuses.

As she had done in other sports, Babe spun tales about her start in golf. In one story, she claimed she had first played five holes with friends and thought the game was stupid. Her favorite tale was that she stopped at a golf course in Dallas and watched folks struggling on the driving range and figured, on the spot, she could "do a lot better than any of them." She strode into the clubhouse, the story went, got some clubs and a bucket of balls, and by the end of the day was hitting them 200 yards, a pretty good distance for a regular, much less a novice. After a few quick tips from the clubhouse pro, she said, her drives improved to as much as 250 yards. "Watching those balls that sailed down there for 200 yards was a sweet feeling," she declared.

It was virtually the exact story line she had used for her experience with the javelin.

Babe's real journey to become a champion golfer was even more extraordinary than her imaginary versions. Her ferocious concentration, her will to succeed, and her raw power served her well on the practice tee and on the fairway. She practiced so relentlessly that golf mentors, competitors, and family were all stunned by her tenacity. Stan Kertes, one of her coaches, watched in awe as she hit 1,500 balls every day off the tee, trying to improve her power and distance. She got to the practice tee "at 9 in the morning and often stayed there 'til the place closed at midnight," he recalled. Admiration turned to worry when Kertes noticed her hands frequently bled from so much work. He made her wear gloves and finally begged her to rest.

How she attached herself to Kertes was revealing. In 1933, in between exhibition gigs, Babe approached Kertes in California, announcing matter-of-factly, "I want to be the greatest woman golfer in the world." In Babe's version of the meeting, Kertes complimented her drive and suggested she take lessons to learn the game's fundamentals. "Yeah," Babe replied, "but it costs too much money." Kertes offered to teach her for free, which was precisely what Babe had hoped. She also managed to get free access to a golf course and driving range. Kertes even bought her a set of clubs.

They had mutual admiration for each other. He invited her back day after day for their grueling practice regimen. They had only been playing together one week when Kertes whacked a very long drive. Babe approached her ball and crushed it, sending it flying thirty yards farther than his. Kertes knew right then she had the makings of a champion. Throughout the spring and summer of 1933, Kertes tutored her until her money ran out. In the years ahead, she returned to him for brush-up lessons as often as she could.

In 1935, the sportswriters Grantland Rice and Paul Gallico intervened to help Babe's golf game and reputation. They were an odd pair to have as allies: Rice, the producer of her staged sports films, had always been supportive and kind, but Gallico repeatedly was cruel in print, a purveyor of hurtful rumors about Babe. It was he who had dubbed her a "muscle moll." Whether he regretted his earlier nastiness or simply stood to profit economically, he, along with Rice, convinced Gene Sarazen, the finest male golfer of the time, to do an exhibition tour with Babe. It was still totally unacceptable for an unmarried woman to travel alone with a man, however. To avoid scandal, Mary Sarazen, Gene's wife, traveled with them as their chaperone.

Sarazen was the biggest name in golf. He won all the major championships: the U.S. Open and Professional Golf Association (PGA) championships, the British Open and Masters, again and again. At the top of his game, universally respected, he was sure to draw huge galleries.

Gene was among the many who was impressed—and even a little disturbed—by Babe's never-ending practice sessions. After they had played eighteen holes, she practiced for hours more, sometimes twelve to sixteen hours per day on weekends. During the work week, she practiced mornings from 5:30 to 8:30 before going to work. She spent their lunch hours putting balls into a leather chair. After work, she took lessons for an hour and practiced until dark. Babe admitted that she pushed herself to the extreme, believing her entire future depended on her ability as a golfer.

Sarazen had opinions about Babe too. He said that it wasn't only the love of golf that brought out the fans. "People wanted to come out and see this freak from Texas who could play golf, tennis, and beat everyone swimming up and down the pool," he said. Her golf skills were remarkable, he noted. Even knowing how much she practiced, he still thought she had a "natural swing," was "strong as an ox," and "physically perfectly built, a real specimen."

In between their exhibition matches, Babe tapped Sarazen's expertise as a tutor. She peppered him with questions. Babe explained that "if I was going to be the best, I wanted to learn from the best." When they scheduled a lesson, Babe would call the local newspaper and tell them when and where it would take place. She made calls to generate publicity in matches against local pros too. When she played against Chicago golf pro Bob McDonald, the caption under her picture read, "On Upswing Again: Queen of athletic femininity, a virtual nobody now, Babe Didrikson follows the club's upswing for an anticipated comeback in golf." If she couldn't rustle up a worthy opponent, Babe just called the local press to tell them she would be on the course, in case they wanted to observe her.

Babe learned how to work her charm on the gallery crowd. Most golfers preferred a quiet, serious, almost reverent atmosphere as they contemplate a shot. Not Babe. In one instance, she attributed her determination to her square jaw. "It's more like a Texas Ranger's jaw than anything else," she joked. "And those rangers were hot when the going was tough."

She loved the electricity the fans' rapport inspired and, as usual, played to the crowd. She joked with reporters, put on the thickest East Texas accent she could muster, and made fun of her own less-than-gorgeous features. She kidded them that "the biggest weakness in my game is that I have too much fun with the galleries. I give the gallery a run for its money." During their exhibitions, Sarazen graciously tolerated her antics. But during competitive matches, opponents found her behavior in poor taste; it contradicted the usual placidity of golf etiquette.

As always, Babe had a series of one-liners. After their lengthy introductions over the loudspeaker, Babe would drawl loudly, "Well, can we play now?" And when an errant shot took her ball into the trees, she exclaimed with a twinkle, "Well, there must be a bottle of Scotch over there in those bushes." Then she would disappear into them. When she had hit a particularly accurate and powerful drive, she would turn to the folks, hands on her hips, and say, "How'm I doin'?" Gradually, she was adding charisma to a sport that was too often filled with boring personalities.

Babe made big money on the 1935 tour with Sarazen—around $250 per match and up. They played eighteen times. Her paydays were supplemented by a newly signed endorsement contract with P. Goldsmith Sons Sporting Goods Company. She agreed to use only their equipment. In return, it would carry her name. This arrangement netted Babe $25,000 a year. At least for the time being, Babe was economically flush, improving her golf game, and getting positive press coverage.

Babe's enthusiasm by summer's end was at a high point. "That Gene made a golfer out of me," she said. "Now I'm on the right track." But just as she began to regain confidence in her relationship with the public, the name-calling began again.

The Texas State Women's Golf Championship was being held at the River Oaks Country Club in Houston. River Oaks was the plushest residential area in Houston, and it hosted the event at its exclusive and refined country club. When Babe registered to compete, Peggy Chandler, a member of the Texas Women's Golf Association, made it clear that Babe was not welcome. "We really don't need any truck drivers' daughters in our tournament." With these unkind words stinging her ears, Babe witnessed more golfers withdraw from a pre-tournament driving contest because of her. They said Babe was too masculine to compete against women. What went unsaid was that they rejected Babe's social class origins as well.

Someone else might have responded with anger, withdrawn from the tournament, or turned her pain inward. Babe responded with humor. Determined to compete, she pretended to be ultra-girlish. During the driving contest, she pranced and preened and took ridiculous swings. If these "rich dames" thought she was manly, then she would poke fun at their idea of femininity. She kept clowning, getting serious only long enough to wallop the ball. One drive went 250 yards. She won the driving contest.

Next came the tournament itself, where she handily defeated her first three challengers. In a dramatic conclusion worthy of Hollywood, the championship came down to Babe and Peggy Chandler, who had been so quick to put Babe down. They played head to head for two complete games, thirty-six holes. The press encouraged Babe because they identified more with her than with the "high society misses." Paul Gallico commented, "The Texas Babe seems to be working out a lifelong vendetta on sissy girls."

Chandler and Babe were tied after thirty holes. At times the course was silent and tense; at others, Babe broke the silence with quips to the fans. At the thirty-fourth hole it seemed Chandler would take the lead. But Babe recovered from a wild tee shot that had put her ball in a ditch and then hit it out of an inch of rainwater in a rut. Miraculously, her third shot went into the cup with a clatter, giving her a score of an eagle three. (Shooting an eagle is two below the par for a hole.) They tied the thirty-fifth hole, and Babe won the thirty-sixth, winning the game and the match.

The gallery went wild, chanting Babe's name. It had been years since she had shone like this in a real competition. Immediately the myths took over. "The tom-boy girl took up golf only two years ago. She went out on the green and found it 'fun to sock 'em and see how far they would go,'" one story said. *Newsweek* jumped immediately on her bandwagon with the headline, "Best at Everything Babe Garners Another Trophy."

Babe was elated. She had risen above pre-tournament

name-calling to become the popular favorite. At this point in her life, she rarely chose to meet conflicts head-on as she had as a streetwise kid. Instead, she relied on her sense of humor in difficult times. In this confrontation with Chandler, Babe sidestepped what could have been an ugly public battle. But her elation was short-lived. Soon afterward, the United States Golf Association (USGA) banned her from amateur competition because she had been paid to compete in other sports. This decision implied that women's amateur golfers did not want any "truck drivers' daughters" trying to earn a living. Only women who were supported financially by their well-off husbands or families were welcome.

Babe's allies rallied on her behalf to overturn the decision. Her supporters called the USGA decision a "bad mistake," a "big joke," and a "dirty deal." For the second time, Babe became a sympathetic underdog held back by officialdom's red tape. She dared not anger national golf officials. If she did, it would ultimately hurt her own aspirations. The USGA had yet to decide if it would bar her for one or three years. If she accepted no money during that time, she would have her amateur status "restored."

The USGA officials decided on a three-year ban. So Babe turned professional. If they would not let her compete with the best amateur golfers, then she would find a way to earn a living as a professional golfer. Her public announcement was mild and carefully worded, even complimentary. "Of course, I was disappointed when they told me I couldn't compete as an amateur," she stated flatly, "but I admire them for barring me too. They were big enough to adhere to their rules." In reality, the USGA's decision was a tough blow, because Babe wanted to improve her game by challenging the excellent amateur players.

Babe hated the constant commentary about her looks, so she decided to change. She took every opportunity to announce that she was a woman and made the public think she was proud of it. "Golf was a woman's game," she said years later, because it was "a game of coordination, rhythm, and grace. Women have this to a much higher degree than men, as dancing shows." In the past, Babe had gone out of her way to separate herself from other women. Now, it was more in her interest to align herself with them because it made her appear to embrace typical "women's interests."

Babe's own deliberate efforts to become feminine were hastened tremendously when she met Bertha Bowen, one of the managers of women's golf in Texas in the fall of 1935. Bertha and her husband, R. L., were prominent Dallasites who had no children. They treated Babe as if she were their own daughter. So much of Babe's life in the last several years had been spent away from home, without the comfort and protection of daily parental love. The Bowens offered her this, and she brought excitement, love, laughter, and limitless possibilities for new experiences into their lives.

Bertha arranged for Babe to meet Texas' best promoters of women's golf, Bea Thompson, and her attorney husband. They could not undo the USGA's ruling; instead, they decided to create a whole new tournament in which Babe could compete. They transformed the Forth Worth Invitational into the Texas Women's Open for both amateurs and professionals. (There was only one other professional match until that time for women.) This meant all the best women golfers of the era could register, and they did. The field of players was illustrious. It included Betsy Rawls, Peggy Kirk Bell, Patty Berg, and Helen Dettweiler. Babe played poorly, but it was a turning point for her. It taught her that she could rely upon the Bowens for help, and it showed her that with cleverness and the right connections, there might be a paying future in women's golf after all.

The Bowens became Babe's surrogate family. She competed against R. L. at billiards. They went boating together and fished by the hour. To Babe, they were "like a godmother and godfather." Because of their trusting bond, Babe felt safe to follow Bertha's lessons in how to become a lady: how to dress for important occasions and how to be polite and more genteel. Bertha taught her patiently, with humor and love, to conform to social class and gender rules. She never criticized Babe. Bertha often said that Babe "was eager to be proper," and she gladly served as Babe's "etiquette guide." She explained why telling ribald stories and jokes might hurt her image. Most important, Bertha showed Babe how to look feminine—and Babe tolerated the lessons.

To use a Texas metaphor, Bertha was trying to break Babe, a wild pony, into accepting a saddle. It was a continuous struggle. Bertha took Babe to Neiman-Marcus, an exclusive and expensive clothing store in Dallas. They bought $700 worth of new clothes for Babe. Bertha introduced Babe to hairstyling and applying makeup and nail polish. Babe followed orders, but drew the line when Bertha tried to squeeze her into a girdle. Girdles are elastic, tight-fitting, tummy-hugging panties that come halfway down the thigh. They were considered necessary wear for most women and were widely sold in department stores. They made women's stomach, buttocks, and thighs slimmer and firmer by tightly holding everything "in place." In fact, the Texas Women's Golf Association had taken Bertha aside and informed her bluntly that "Babe really must wear a girdle when she plays golf." Bertha, patient as always, explained this required feminine gear to Babe.

Once, just once, Babe complied with the regulation. She played a round of golf in the restrictive undergarment. Then, frenzied, she raced back to the Bowens' home. Bertha heard the car screech into the driveway. Babe dashed into the house, yelling, "Goddamn! I'm chokin' to death!" Bertha said, "As far as I know, she never put on a girdle again."

Bertha, R. L., and Babe collaborated on a public image for Babe, but when she was alone with the Bowens, she could be herself. She wore shorts, talked in her East Texas slang, and indulged in her own rather peculiar food preferences: pork and beans, chewy banana candy, and of course, onion sandwiches and strawberry sodas. It was as if she were playing a part when she was out of the house.

On a personal level, the Bowens delighted in her fierce competitive streak and endless pranks. Once on a fishing trip to their lakeside cabin in Colorado, R. L. and Babe wagered $10 on who could catch the biggest fish. They went their separate ways and agreed to meet at noon to compare their catches. R. L. and Bertha were delighted when they landed a big fish. For once, they thought, they would actually beat the Babe at something. But Babe came trotting in, hip boots on, with what Bertha thought was "the biggest trout you can imagine, and it don't even grow in that river!" They never did figure out where Babe got the monster fish; she probably bought it.

Throughout the 1940s and 1950s, Bertha kept an eye on and monitored Babe's appearance. On more than one occasion, she lent Babe a dress to wear while competing in a golf tournament because she knew the public would see Babe's choice as unacceptable. Babe even came to expect similar transformations for other tomboy women. Betty Dodd, who was later part of Babe's chosen family, said that Babe gave her hair a permanent. Betty was resisting the tight curlers and Babe kept screaming at her, "Sit still! Bertha made a lady out of me and I'm gonna do the same thing to you!"

Delighted with her new image, Babe summoned her critics. When Paul Gallico interviewed her, he was flabbergasted by her makeover. "I hardly knew Babe Didrikson when I saw her," he wrote. "Hair frizzed and she had a neat little wave in it, parted and prettily combed, a touch of rouge on her cheeks and red on her lips. The tomboy," he declared, "had suddenly grown up."

Babe went so far as to offer Gallico "proof" of her crossover into womanhood. When they met up at an Ohio golf tournament, she "shyly, with infinite femininity," confessed, "I got 'em," and lifted the hem of her golf skirt "to disclose the silk-and-lace garment beneath." After showing him her slip, she opened her purse so he could see her lipstick, compact, eye shadow, and lace hanky. Gallico announced to his millions of readers that Babe was, at last, a normal woman.

Babe might have gone to all that fuss just to prove she was "normal," but she ended the interview with a thick put-on Texas drawl: "Ah got tired of being a tomboy, so ah quit. Ah'm a businesswoman golfer now, so ah guess ah hayev to look th' part." How could wearing a slip and a little makeup truly change who she was? It didn't. Inside Babe had felt "normal" all along! She would act the part, but it didn't really match who she was at heart.

Years later, Babe went even further. She wrote fictional stories in her autobiography about her boyfriends at Beaumont High and while she was competing with the ECC in Dallas. Two boys fought each other for her affections, she wrote. She noted she had more than one marriage proposal. She turned them down because "I was too busy working on my sports career."

Babe rewrote her real life story deliberately, but she sacrificed her own authentic past by doing so. She did not want anyone to question whether she was "all female." In her later years, she even cautioned girl athletes not to "get tough" competing against boys. The irony was that she was condemning her own contests against both boys and men—contests that had helped make her an exceptional athlete. Her self-esteem depended on acting like someone other than who she really was, and she actively squelched parts of herself that were different. Her tough edge and man-woman appearance had been empowering and unique for her. Though she had been comfortable that way, that Babe was now eliminated outside the walls of her home.

ELEVEN

Domestic Bliss?

In 1938, at the Los Angeles Open Golf Tournament, Babe met George Zaharias, a handsome, athletic, professional wrestler. They were made for each other—or so it seemed.

It was not a great time in Babe's life. Her career was floundering; her tour with Sarazen had been over for a long time, and she was flat broke once again. The Los Angeles Open was a tournament for professional and amateur men only. But desperate to get publicity and practice her game, Babe registered. It was a clever ploy. No rule actually forbade a woman from competing in it.

A local sports promoter teamed up Babe with a Presbyterian minister and the wrestler whose "tag name" in the ring was the "Crying Greek from Cripple Creek." (He came from Cripple Creek, Colorado.) Babe was twenty-seven,

George thirty-nine. The two of them had several things in common. Like Babe, George was the child of immigrant parents: Gus and Demitra Vetoyanis, from Tripoli, Greece. George's birth name was Theodore; he had Americanized his name, as Babe and other children of immigrants had done. He was also from a working-class background. His father had been a steel mill worker who became a farmer in Colorado. Like Babe, George struck out on his own as a teen in the hope of bettering his and his family's future.

George decided to capitalize on his body—235 pounds of solid muscle. Babe described him as "husky and black-haired and handsome." Like Babe, he created a public image for himself so interesting that people would pay to see him perform in the ring. He had a hard time breaking into wrestling at first. He was competing with hundreds of immigrant boys with the same dreams. But clever George knew he had to be an attraction as well as an athlete. Wrestling at that time was much like today, part theater and part athletics. To be successful, a wrestler had to safely tumble, hurl himself through the air, and perform many other feats on cue. Popular wrestlers also had an identifiable personality that the audience either adored or hated.

George presented himself as a villain. As soon as he appeared in the ring, the crowd booed and hissed at him. He flexed his biceps and made faces or pouted at the audience. The nicknames he used as a wrestler reflect some of his stage characters: Gorgeous George Zaharias, the Colorado Crooner, the Pueblo Pouter, and the Meanest Man.

George and Babe shared several other key traits. He longed for media attention because it led to more matches and the promise of a paycheck. He promoted himself relentlessly. He was flamboyant and entertaining. Like Babe, he was popular precisely because of his controversial—and often unlikable—persona. "The fans hate me, but pay money to see me wrestle, probably in the hope I'll get my neck broken," he explained. While he whined, grunted, and scowled, he also used "dirty tricks." He poked competitors in the eye, punched them, elbowed and kicked them in the head when they were down—all illegal moves. No wonder audiences hated him. And George, too, bragged about and predicted his victories.

When not acting out his nasty "Crying Greek" ring routine, he endeared himself to reporters. One writer described him as "the kind of guy you felt like giving a big cookie to, a big shambling bear with cauliflowered ears." Acquaintances said he had an attractive personality: friendly, boisterous, a booming laugh, "a clever story teller, easy to interview, speaks first-class English." These were almost the exact same words used to describe Babe.

Like Babe, George also had parlayed his clownish athletic skills into a greatly improved life for his family. He had already built a home for his parents, funded the education of his two younger brothers, Chris and Tom, and provided "seed money" for two brothers-in-law to open businesses. George looked like the ultimate in masculinity: tough and powerful, unafraid, and able to take physical punishment. Since Babe had become more subdued and soft in public, she complimented his aggressive and rough image. But at their first meeting, George was disappointed. "I didn't want to go out there with a girl, no matter what girl," he said. Despite his misgivings, friends convinced Big George to tee off with his assigned teammates at 11 that morning.

Both George and Babe said it was love—or at least physical attraction—at first sight. "When we shook hands, a big thrill went through me. In a minute, I had my arms around her, showing her wrestling holds for the press photographers," he recalled. "There were cameras all around us and it seemed to me there was electricity all around us. I couldn't get my eyes filled up with her. It was wonderful."

George won that day's golf match: he shot an 82, she shot an 83. Had Babe intentionally lost the match by one stroke because it was unseemly for a woman to beat the man she liked? Perhaps she was worried about his ego, and she did not want to frighten George away with her superior golf game. Or had she legitimately lost? One thing was certain: George left that day smitten with Babe. They each looked forward to their second round the next day.

Their courtship began immediately. In George, Babe found the "normal" relationship that the public always wanted her to have. She also found an attentive, charismatic, and willing beau. After the second day's round was over, George invited Babe for a grilled steak dinner at the apartment he shared with his brothers. Before dinner, George called for Babe at her apartment where he briefly met Hannah and Lillie, her temporary guests. It pleased Babe greatly that "Momma liked him straight off." Hannah also was pleased at George's request to take Babe dancing after dinner. "He's a nice man," she said.

It was not a typical first date, but one that suited Babe just fine. At the apartment, Chris and Tom each showed off their wrestling holds on Babe while George cooked. George nicknamed Babe "Romance," and she said of him, "I always said I could fall in love with a man strong enough to outdrive me" in golf.

Both sets of relatives approved of their match. No doubt George's parents reminded Babe of Hannah and Olé, and vice versa. Both sets of parents were sheltered by their native language and customs, in addition to being lavishly provided for by their successful children.

Her relationship with George, which was splashed across newspapers nationwide, earned Babe complete acceptance as a "real" woman. Gallico, always ready to chart Babe's life, wrote, "Until the Babe met and married . . . George Zaharias . . . she was a pathetic and solitary figure, neither one thing nor another in the average, normal world of ordinary men or women or even, for that matter, of athletes." Surely Babe was hurt by that assessment, but she could balance that criticism with pride in her accomplishments. She was too busy earning a living, practicing her golf, and enjoying all life had to offer to feel "pathetic."

Their mutual affection grew, but their athletic obligations frequently kept them apart. Once, when Babe, Hannah, and Lillie set out by car to visit sister Dora in Phoenix, Babe became fed up with her constant separation from George. She got to Phoenix, unloaded her family, and drove back to be with George. When she arrived at his apartment, she learned he had left for San Francisco for a wrestling match. Determined to surprise him, Babe coerced Chris, George's brother, to drive the 460 miles with her through the night. The weary travelers arrived at the St. Marks Hotel, where the wrestlers were lodging. In a scene worthy of a movie reunion, Babe pounded her fists on George's door. When he threw open the door to see who was making all that racket, he threw out his arms, beamed, and said, "Come here, Romance." He gave her a big kiss, and she recalled, "Then I wasn't lonesome anymore."

No question they were in love. For the first time in her adult life, Babe felt she could depend on someone else's strength and judgment. The prospects of building a permanent home and of sharing her daily life with someone who knew and understood her were wonderfully appealing.

Everything in her life to that point had fostered a strong sense of independence, self-reliance, and clarity of purpose. The relationship with George meant she had a chance to share life with someone who was as much a rugged individual as she was. It's most likely that together they created the impression that Babe was "the little woman" and he the strong protective male. It suited their personal goals and their career aspirations.

They announced their engagement in St. Louis on July 22, 1938. But their wedding was postponed repeatedly because of their professional obligations, and this inability to arrange matters in order to say their vows foreshadowed things to come. The time they spent together was rare and contentious.

Six months elapsed after they announced their engagement; still they could not find a free date. Finally, George presented Babe with an ultimatum: "Get married this week or call the deal off."

Without any family members in attendance, they wed in St. Louis in January 1939, one year after they had met. Their simple wedding was anticlimactic. It was held in the home of George's friend, a wrestling promoter, and presided over by a Greek judge. Leo Durocher, baseball player and personality, served as George's best man, and Leo's wife, Grace, stood up for Babe.

Thus, Babe became Mrs. George Zaharias. There was no time for a honeymoon. They each had matches booked, so they went back to earning a living.

Even though their marriage began "on the fly," Babe

hoped they would soon have a quiet home life. At first, it seemed as if her dream might be realized. They settled in Los Angeles and rented a duplex with a yard near some of George's business investments. George portrayed these early months of their marriage as harmonious and full of comforting decorating sessions and hours spent at home. "Right away she was a housewife," he said. "She bought furniture—big overstuffed chairs I could sit in." George's savings financed their home. While this might have been a relief to Babe, it was also an end to the autonomy that she had always enjoyed. She had not saved any money, and George's opinions, if they disagreed, always overruled hers.

George was a loving but dominating husband, who believed that the man should be the ruler in the home. This was a typical attitude of their generation. He promoted Babe constantly, setting up appearances for her that guaranteed a few bucks here and there and arranging a travel schedule for both of them that produced lengthy separations. Babe had little or no choice in the matter.

However, Babe quickly grew very unhappy with these developments. After years of barnstorming through town after town, she wanted to be more settled. She enjoyed George's companionship when they were together. But she was bitterly disappointed when she realized she was still eating meals alone in diners and staying in hotels by herself, then traveling in darkness to her next assigned appearance. For the first time, she felt helpless. By surrendering all her power to George, she had lost control of her own life.

In April 1939, George announced to Babe that they were booked for a honeymoon trip to Hawaii. To Babe's disappointment, he had arranged numerous wrestling matches for himself and golf exhibitions for her. Babe had wanted a more

private, leisurely celebration, but George insisted that she fulfill the commitments he had arranged. It marked George's
start as Babe's professional manager. "Sweetheart, husband,
manager, adviser"—that was how he described himself.

He branched out beyond the United States and its pos-
sessions, booking a tour of Australia. In part, this was to
please Babe, who was fascinated with the continent and
wanted to visit. It was also a brilliant career move. There
were too few tournaments in which she could compete in
America. So George "borrowed" successful hustling ploys
from his wife by booking her against prominent male pros.
She would entertain the public while polishing her game.
The exhibitions generated money, fans, and press coverage
and introduced George worldwide as her husband-manager-
business partner. When they merged their promotional abilities, they were truly impressive and effective.

After months of travel they returned home in the fall of
1939. Babe was pleased with her improved golf game and
positive press. But she was also weary and discouraged. Her
married life had her on the move as much as her single life
had, and still, her future in competitive golf looked dim. As
she herself said of that period, "Here I'd been practicing all
the time and developed this fine golf game, and about all I
could do was play exhibition matches. I wasn't getting a
chance to show whether I was the best woman's player
because I was barred from practically all the women's tournaments as a professional."

George, who shared Babe's frustration on golf matters,
then made two decisions that turned around both Babe's
golf career and their marriage. He had invested his
wrestling earnings well and had become a licensed wrestling
promoter, who lined up matches for others, rented the halls,

advertised, and sold tickets. Some matches were championships, which brought even bigger paydays. He was making enough money so they could live off his earnings, while Babe refused any paid work for three years. This would allow her to regain her amateur standing and begin to compete in the available women's tournaments. Babe was thrilled.

George's second decision also pleased her. He withdrew from wrestling as an athlete and turned his energies toward Babe's career. George had been hurt more than once and Babe feared for his safety and health. Sure, wrestling stunts and moves were choreographed in advance or feigned, but even so, repeated body slams, jolts to the back, kidneys and head, and wrenched limbs had taken their toll. Typically, in this era, it was the wife who gave up her pursuits to concentrate on her husband's career. But in this couple, it was obvious who had the greater stardom. So Babe's career took center stage—with George at the helm. He was, he said, "dedicating myself to her and letting her do what she wanted." Well, not all she wanted.

It was true that Babe longed to regain her amateur standing. Under George's guidance she secured the four letters signed by prominent golf amateurs endorsing her request to be reinstated. They submitted her application in early 1940. The United States Golf Association (USGA), Babe said, "agreed to restore my amateur standing if I went through the three-year waiting period. I settled down to sweat it out," she said later. When she did enter occasional open tournaments, she told promoters "count me out on any prize money."

It was a difficult adjustment. Now economically dependent on George, Babe was both grateful for the opportunity and distressed by it. Controlling and earning her own money had been a focus of her life. But the autonomy that her own income gave her was gone. What is more, this impatient woman was hardly accustomed to waiting for anything. Three years! It felt like it would last forever.

She coped as best she could, with a little golf and a lot of a sport she had not played much, tennis. In 1940, at age twenty-nine, Babe devoted herself to making the best possible showing in the only two golf tournaments for which she was eligible: the Western Women's Open in Milwaukee, Wisconsin, and the Texas Women's Open at Fort Worth— the one Bertha had "created" for Babe years before. She captured both, and they gave her the momentum she needed. They gave her a "little slam," she said. Now she could hardly wait to begin battling for all the top championships.

As for tennis, Babe went all out, of course. The shoulder that had been injured in the Olympic javelin throw was healed. George lined up lessons with top coach Eleanor "Teach" Tennant at the Beverly Hills Tennis Club. Babe showed no restraint in learning this new game, playing sixteen or seventeen sets a day. "There was hardly a day when I didn't wear holes in my socks," she recalled.

Within a few months, Babe was regularly beating not only her tennis teacher, but also prominent male film stars and leading women tennis players as well. It was all for naught. In the fall of 1941, Babe tried to register for the Pacific Southwest Tennis Tournament, only to learn she was barred from this sport as well. The rules declared that once someone became a professional in any sport, she was a professional in tennis too. It was another crushing setback. Without the lure of top-notch competition, Babe abandoned tennis immediately. She was never one to take up a sport to merely have fun or stay fit.

What next? Babe was like a firefly trapped in a lidded jar. George, who had considered buying a bowling alley as an investment, decided Babe should try bowling. She began to spend hours on it every night. Bowling's rules allowed Babe to compete as an amateur. Finally! In her first hundred games, she regularly reached scores of 200 and once bowled 268. (A perfect game of all strikes is 300.) She led her King's Jewelry team of Southern California to a league championship. For nearly two years, bowling kept Babe sane. George worried that repeatedly hurling the fourteen-pound ball would overstrengthen her right arm and cause her to hook her golf shots, but this never happened.

But Babe wanted golf. Since she couldn't compete for money, she actually entered tournaments for the sheer joy of playing. In 1941, she won the Women's Open in San Francisco. Real contests remained hard to come by, so she often had to settle for meaningless practice rounds. Even in these, she went all out, scoring a club record 64 at the Brentwood Country Club. She also won an alternate shot match—one in which two team members take turns taking every other shot—with the great male golfer, Sam Snead.

George also arranged exhibition matches in which Babe was paired with comedian Bob Hope and singer Bing Crosby, both avid golfers. "There's only one thing wrong about Babe and myself. I hit the ball like a girl and she hits it like a man," Hope wisecracked afterward.

However, once the United States entered World War II, even celebrity golf tournaments were scarce. So Babe played in charity tournaments to benefit the military effort. Among her opponents: film star Mickey Rooney and Olympic swimming gold medallist Johnny Weismuller, who won fame in the movies as Tarzan. She even played golf against the man she called "the Big Babe," Babe Ruth.

Another wartime project was community involvement in Denver, where Babe and George had recently moved to be nearer George's various businesses and family. She was appointed as a probation officer and recreational consultant by the city. Denver officials thought she was a great role model for children. For her efforts, which included teaching baseball, swimming, and golf to children in detention and orphanages, she received a symbolic key to the city.

As Babe's prospects increased, George's prospects, beyond being her husband-manager, decreased. Within a few years of their marriage, George's fame and fortune depended totally upon his manipulation of Babe's career. She tried to boost his ego. "George is the business head of the family," she declared to anyone who would listen. But they had sacrificed a part of themselves that was important for their self-esteem. George lost his own identity to put Babe in the spotlight; Babe lost her economic independence and the power to chart her own course.

She tried to emphasize the positive side. "All the while I was enjoying being Mrs. George Zaharias. That's what I've been ever since we were married, whether I was keeping house or playing in a golf tournament," she declared. "I always competed as Mrs. Zaharias, not Babe Didrikson. We're a team." In her new incarnation as a middle-class housewife, she even asked one reporter to call her Mildred, not Babe, since it was more feminine.

Finally, early in 1945, she was able to reenter competitive women's golf. But she suffered a devastating blow later the same year. Babe regained her amateur status in time to compete in a charity match against the California State women's champion, Clara Callender. Babe beat Callender by five strokes and set a course record of 67 in the process. Shortly thereafter, the two teed off again in the Midwinter Women's Golf Championship at the Los Angeles County Club. Babe won again.

In June, Babe was defending her Western Women's Open title in Indianapolis when George called with awful news. Hannah, a diabetic, had suffered a heart attack and was hospitalized. Babe was devastated. She wanted to return immediately to Beaumont to be at Hannah's bedside, but George and her sister Nancy urged her to continue in the competition. They told her repeatedly, "Your momma wants you to finish the tournament." In addition, it was virtually impossible to get an airline ticket from Indianapolis because the military commandeered most of the seats.

Torn, Babe stayed in Indianapolis. "A lot of times I'd have to step away and wipe my eyes before I could putt," she recalled later. She won her semifinal match, only to receive the phone call she had been dreading. It was Nancy. Hannah was dead.

Heartbroken, Babe tried to get a seat on a plane. When she failed, Nancy said. "You go ahead and win that tournament. That's the way Momma would want it." Babe resigned herself to continue. As was so often the case, she was alone; George was off on business. That night, to distract herself from her despair, Babe invited two golfers to dinner with her. Peggy Kirk Bell and Marge Row lent silent companionship to a distraught Babe. Bell recalled finding Babe sitting in her room, playing her harmonica. "We didn't really know her and didn't know what to say," Bell recollected. "She played for hours."

Babe dedicated her final match to Hannah. She really

didn't have her heart in it, but she beat Dorothy Germain by six strokes anyway. At 5 the next morning, she secured a seat on a plane. But because of the distance and war needs, Babe was forced to give up her seat and disembark several times. It took two grueling days for Babe to reach home.

Hannah's death devastated her. She hoped George's companionship would help heal her loss, but they grew further apart.

TWELVE

Superman's Sister

With her amateur status reinstated, Babe was ready to devour her competitors. She had been forced to put it off long enough. Golf offered Babe exactly what she wanted. She aspired to wealth, and golf had always been an elite sport of the upper social classes. A woman needed money to buy a set of clubs, pay club membership dues and course fees, tip a caddie, and she needed leisure time to play eighteen holes often enough to become skilled. Amateur rules had allowed women to compete as early as 1893, albeit reluctantly, and because society women played golf, there were practically never any rumors that they were not feminine enough.

Once she rejoined the top players in 1945, Babe's style revolutionized women's golf. Previously, women took restricted, ladylike, graceful swings at the ball. Babe smashed it with a grace that came from power, and she drove the ball as long as men did. She played to win, to set records, and to capture big purses. *Sports Illustrated* summed up her contribution by saying, "Babe Zaharias created big-time women's golf. She launched it as a legitimate sport and brought gusts of freshness and fun to a game too often grim." Her booming power game lowered scores and forced others to imitate her.

Babe became famous for her 250-yard drives off the tee. This was something that few female pros and fewer amateurs could do. Her short game (those shots hit near the green) was also excellent. One writer noted that she "could chip the ball to the pin and sink 20-foot putts as easily as she could slam the ball 275 yards." She also studied golf's rulebook religiously, sometimes climbing into bed with it after dinner. "I'll bet," she said, "I have read that book through twenty-five times, line by line."

Amazingly, she could maintain her concentration even while clowning with the fans. Many thought Babe's wit, charm, and teasing one-liners violated golf's strict etiquette, but Babe thought differently, and her popularity with the galleries gave her still another psychological edge over her opponents. The crowd's cheering helped her play better. Naturally, she received the lion's share of press coverage, regardless of who won.

Stories of her golf course antics became legendary in her lifetime and are still retold today. She put on dazzling displays of trick shots. In one, she launched five balls so quickly the fifth would be airborne before the first landed. Or she would shoot left-handed (she was a natural righty). She could make balls "jump" over her outstretched foot into the cup.

She would keep up a steady patter of flippant lines, like "Stand back caddie! This ain't no kid hittin'," or "Watch close, boys, 'cause you're watchin' the best." Sometimes when she was having a bad day, she reverted to her thick Texas twang and drawled, "Ah couldn't hit an elephant's ass with a bull fiddle today." Her brassy attitude rattled opponents and bothered those who guarded golf's etiquette. When she saw someone bristle, Babe would crank her antics up a notch. One of her favorite ways to annoy the high-society folks was to flip a cigarette in the air, catch it in her mouth, and light the match with her thumbnail. As the grandes dames rolled their eyes, the crowed cheered. Once she went so far as to gather a group of golfers around her so she could remove her slip in the middle of the match on a hot day. She tossed it to her caddie in front of 3,000 fans, much to the chagrin of some stuffy clubhouse patrons. She used one crowd-pleasing line often: "When I wanta really bust one, I just loosen my girdle and let 'er fly!"

She had all kinds of ways to psych out other players. Once, when she was down by several strokes late in a match, Babe attached several children's exploding pistol caps to her ball. She swung her club and when it hit the ball, the hefty explosion jarred everyone's nerves so badly that Babe went on to win.

In the locker room, Babe tried to reduce her competitors to Jell-O. "Hi, girls!" she shouted as she entered a tournament locker room. "Ya gonna stick around and see who'll finish second this week?" Once she called together a group of players to announce that she was the star and they were just the "spear carriers," and "no one paid to see spear toters." She taunted everyone, alienating the other golfers.

In her own mind, her behavior was not only excusable but ultimately beneficial to all. When crowds and the press came to see her, she reasoned, every player's economic opportunities increased. More people and more coverage meant that more sponsors would offer more prize money. Neither her banter nor her pranks, however, endeared her to her challengers.

Throughout 1945, she dominated women's golf. She won the Texas Women's Open title, the Western Open, and challenge matches at Los Angeles and San Antonio, and she was chosen Woman Athlete of the Year in the annual Associated Press poll. This honor, coming thirteen years after being picked the first time, meant the world to Babe. As 1945 came to a close, she was established as golf's ruling queen.

Babe returned to her pattern of predicting great exploits. "I want to establish the longest winning streak in the history of women's golf," she said in 1946. And starting in August 1946, she won thirteen consecutive amateur tournaments. Before some matches, she even guessed the exact score she would shoot that day. On the rare occasion when she was correct, she posed for the cameras in front of the scoreboard gesturing proudly that she had been right. She became more famous with every photo.

Her first and second victories were in Denver and Colorado Springs. Then she won the All-American Championship in Niles, Illinois, followed by the U.S. Women's Amateur national championship in Tulsa, Oklahoma. Her fifth consecutive victory was the Texas Women's Open. She closed out 1946 undefeated. No golfer before or since has been able to repeat this accomplishment.

Babe was in the midst of perhaps the most astounding winning streak in the history of sports. But now she was tired and homesick. George insisted, though, that she continue on the circuit, especially since he was partly responsible for the streak. In October, after five tournaments, he had told her, "You want to build that streak up into a record they'll never forget. There are some women's tournaments in Florida at the start of the winter. I think you should go down there."

Babe wanted to go home in Denver and rest. "No way," said George. He wanted to make sure she made good on her promise. She pleaded with him to accompany her so they could have a couple's life on the road. At first he agreed, but then he broke his promise and sent her alone to the next tournament. They argued, but George prevailed. Once again she slept in a different hotel each night, ate by herself in diners, and drove endless miles, twirling the radio dial for any station that would cheer her. This was not her idea of marriage.

She still played like a champion regardless of what she was feeling inside. Victory six came at the Tampa Women's Open in January 1947. Next came the Helen Lee Doherty Women's Open in Miami. Orlando, Palm Beach, Hollywood, Ormond Beach, St. Augustine—week after week, the record was building. When she notched the Women's Titleholder's Tournament trophy in Georgia, that summer, it was her thirteenth consecutive win.

Then in late August, she finally lost—at the National Open in Spokane, Washington. Perhaps the travel exhausted her, but in Babe's mind, it was a fluke. She resumed her winning ways at a tourney in Pinehurst, North Carolina. From then on, she simply ignored her Spokane loss, calling Pinehurst win number fourteen. She counted her next win at the Celebrities Tournament in Washington as fifteen.

By this time, she was completely worn out. A month loomed before the next tournament. She was "really ready

*Babe proudly points out her score, which she had
successfully predicted, late 1940s.*

to go home and see my flowers and work around the house
and garden." As before, George put pressure on her. "Don't
go home," he said. "Go to Scotland and play in the British
Women's Amateur. You need something like that to top off
your streak," he argued, "the way Bobby Jones went over
and played those British tournaments." No American had
ever won the British Women's Amateur, and it would bring
her invaluable international exposure.

Babe's desire for immortality was as large as George's
dreams for her, so she went. But once again, George didn't
hold up his end of the bargain by going with her. Each time
they quarreled over travel, George would renege and either
stay comfortably ensconced in Denver or roam around on

his own. When it came time to plan the Scotland trip, Babe was fed up. Once again she pleaded with him to accompany her. Once again he lamely said he would try. "I know you. You're giving me some more of that old con," she replied. "You won't go."

She made the ocean voyage alone. What George didn't realize was that he had just made one of the biggest mistakes of their marriage. Babe's solo journey marked a turning point both professionally and personally.

In Scotland, townspeople were gracious and charmed by her. Everywhere she went, townsfolk recognized her and called out hellos, addressing her as "Mrs. Zaharias." Babe told reporters, "I wish you'd ask everybody just to call me Babe."

She was enchanted by local customs. She discovered that in Scotland, sheep wandered freely over the lush, thick grass of the golf courses, and their chewing kept them "mowed." A man walked ahead of her to scoop up the sheep droppings. The courses were nothing like the close-cropped, carpetlike greens she was used to. She worked at adapting to the long, wet grass. During one shot, her club got caught in the growth and the handle banged her thumb. It chipped a bone. As always, Babe determined not to reveal this injury lest it give her opponents a psychological edge. She was single-minded about her mission: to prove she could beat the best women golfers on both sides of the Atlantic.

She had not packed the right clothes to play in the cold Scottish weather, and her teeth chattered during some matches. Wartime rationing prevented her from buying new warm clothes. So she donned a pair of warm pants given to her by local folks. Her secondhand trousers were dubbed by the media as her "lucky pants," or as the Scots called them, her "slocks." Her outfit and its humble origin increased her bond with the hometown fans. It didn't take long before she became the Scottish fans' favorite female golfer.

Babe entertained the practice gallery with her quips, trick shots, spontaneous harmonica tunes, and impromptu steps of the Highland Fling, which she performed in a kilt she had bought specifically to please the tournament hosts. The crowds loved her. She violated staid golf etiquette by letting the fans gather close and engaged them in frequent chitchat. Her shenanigans drew such huge galleries to the tournament that the crowds grew to 8,000 people a day, outnumbering the men's competition.

Winning easily, she was now Europe's favorite as well as America's. After winning the tournament, she spent a few days playing on legendary British golf courses with local male professionals. In two instances, Babe was the first woman allowed into the clubhouses and on the greens. Yet despite her triumphs, she longed to return home. She had already been away from George longer than any other time in their marriage.

Back in New York, the phone rang off the hook with offers. They rejected them all, until Fred Corcoran, the promotional director of the Men's Professional Golf Association, showed up. Then Babe made two momentous decisions. First, she hired Corcoran to represent her. It was an excellent choice. Corcoran represented baseball greats Ted Williams and Stan Musial and golfers Bob Jones and Sam Snead. He had also been the man behind Babe's exhibition tour with Gene Sarazen years earlier. Thus, after nine years of marriage, George would no longer be her solo manager, although to soothe his ego, she agreed to allow both men to book appearances for her. In a second big decision, after a persuasive pitch by Corcoran, Babe decided to turn professional.

In Denver, Babe was greeted with a grand parade and was given a gigantic key to the city. George, still the showman himself, resurrected his old wrestling strongman antics to lift the 250-pound, 15-foot key in his arms. But there was no rest for the weary Babe. She was committed to the Broadmoor Match Play Tournament at Colorado Springs just a few weeks later. She won and called it her seventeenth consecutive amateur win.

In recognition of her astounding winning streak and international fame, Babe, age thirty-six, was voted one of 1947's Women of the Year by the Associated Press. Her stature now surpassed the boundaries of sports. She shared the honor with three other stars: singer Helen Traubel and actresses Helen Hayes and Ingrid Bergman.

As a newly declared professional, Babe was free to accept any money for her time, services, or endorsements. Corcoran booked her in a golfball driving exhibition at major league ballparks and pitted her against the Boston Red Sox's Ted Williams in a driving contest in Sarasota, Florida. One night at New York's Yankee Stadium, after the golf exhibition, she grabbed a glove and started fielding grounders at third base. Corcoran recalled that "she was hobbled somewhat by her skirt, but that didn't phase her. She ripped it up the front and went back to scooping up ground balls and firing them across to first base. The crowd went wild."

Corcoran signed Babe to a lifetime contract with Wilson Sporting Goods. She would promote Babe Zaharias golf equipment for the huge sum of $8,000 a year. Corcoran arranged a second golf equipment endorsement with P. Goldsmith Sons Sporting Goods Company. She also signed with the Serbin dress manufacturers, who made women's golf clothes, and even codesigned a few items: a golf dress, a shirt with buttons on the sleeves to allow for a wider swing, and a golf shoe with removable spikes. Babe described them as "sensible for gals who want comfort with grooming," and she reminded everyone of her prize-winning dress in high school. This contract led to a hefty $10,000 per year deal with Alvin Handmacher, who paid her to wear the clothes he designed for Weathervane sportswear. Babe appeared in magazine advertisements for Timex watches and for Prest-O-Lite, an automobile battery. Like the big male athletes, she also endorsed cigarettes. (This was many years before the deadly health effects of tobacco were publicly known.)

Adding to her coffers were fees from exhibitions. It was fast and easy money—$1,000 for one match. No woman athlete had ever earned so much. Other women golfers were glad for Babe's success because she paved the way for them too, but they also resented the special treatment she received. After all, some of her cohorts did exhibitions free to promote their sport.

It was a good thing Corcoran generated this extra income. In 1948, even though Babe was the leading money winner in professional women's golf, she only earned $3,400 for the entire year from golf tournaments.

It had taken years of plugging, but at last Babe had the wealth and steady income that she had always wanted. As much as Babe reveled in her burgeoning bank account, she continued to hustle folks for "freebie" favors. The Great Depression left an indelible mark on her, as it had on so many Americans. She still delighted in wrangling a deal, and she had come to believe that these items were due her. Babe knew that everyone—from her grocer to her golf apparel supplier—profited by claiming they knew her or by selling her an item. People showered gifts on her so they could be photographed with her or somehow use her name.

She milked her stature for all she was worth. Admirers bought her free meals, one jeweler gave her a free Rolex watch, and she got free lodging and airplane rides when she traveled. When Babe heard that golfer Byron Nelson got a horse from a sponsor, she demanded one as well, and got it. A few Sundays later Babe arrived at Bertha's in Fort Worth pulling a horse trailer.

Under Corcoran's skillful guidance, Babe could afford to pick and choose her endorsements. The money helped soften the regret when her long winning streak ended. Even better, the loss gave Babe an excuse to give up road travel, if only for a few months.

Even with her newfound prosperity, Babe wanted to earn more money from golf itself, not just endorsements. Determined to be tested by top-level challengers, she tried to enter the 1948 men's National Open, but was barred from it as a woman. Having so few playing opportunities was frustrating. Other excellent women golfers felt the same: it was next to impossible for women golfers to earn a living from their sport.

Women needed a professional golf circuit. In 1944 a group of women golfers had organized themselves into a pro group. But it only lasted until 1947 because they could not get enough sponsors. With Babe leading the way, sponsors were finally convinced that enough public interest existed to make a women's pro tour. Babe credited George with beginning the circuit. But the truth was that L. B. Icely, president of Wilson Sporting Goods, contacted Corcoran and asked him to organize the tour. Wilson paid Corcoran's salary, as tour organizer, and Weathervane Sports Clothes Company put up the prize money.

The new association, the Ladies Professional Golf Association (LPGA) was born in 1949, with Patty Berg elected its first president. The six women founders of LPGA had a difficult task in front of them. They had to secure long-term sponsorship funding and balance all their strong and often conflicting personalities.

Babe was one of these women, and George, Babe's sometime agent and constant advisor, did not make these tasks easier. He announced more than once to all the assembled founders that "women's golf belongs to me. It's a racket, golf is, just like the wraslin' and boxin' racket. And it's gotta be run the same way." He was dead wrong. Wrestling matches frequently had "fixed" outcomes where losers knew their role and were paid to take a licking. This was not so with golf. It was an honest competitive game whose winner was determined by skill. Women like Patty Berg and Peggy Kirk Bell had been working just as hard as George and Babe to make golf a sport in which women could earn a living. They had also been fighting for higher prize money. George's heavy-handed approach, combined with Babe's need for center stage, alienated the Zahariases from the other founders.

The others might have been forced to deal with George and Babe, since they needed Babe's personality and name recognition for their success. But the abrasiveness of the Zahariases caused many arguments. That's probably why Berg was reelected president in 1950, 1951, and 1952. Babe served as president between 1953 and 1955.

Everyone, including her opponents, knew Babe was the LPGA's main drawing card. They would have been grateful, however, if Babe had refrained from pointing it out to them at every opportunity. Unfortunately, Babe never tempered her self-promotion with consideration for the feelings of others. It was ironic because she no longer needed to promote herself so persistently. But she continued to insist that everything in the LPGA revolve around her.

Babe dominated the new women's tour. She won nearly a third of the prize money on the tour in 1949. In 1950 she improved upon that; she won two-thirds of the LPGA tournaments, earned $14,000, and was the tour's leading money winner. In 1951, for the second consecutive year, she led the tour in winnings, with $15,087. Despite the personal ambivalence other golfers felt toward her, they elected her to the LPGA Hall of Fame in 1951; it had been established in 1950.

By June 1951, she had maximized her earning power to the point where *Time* magazine called her "Big Business Babe." Her extracurricular activities included some astounding numbers. In a three-year period she had performed 656 exhibitions, roughly one every day and a half. She was paid $500 per round on weekdays and $600 on Sundays. *Time* estimated that she had pulled in about $250,000 from prize money, sporting goods companies, movie and television shorts, endorsements, royalties on equipment bearing her name, plus investments.

The lean young woman from the dusty streets of East Texas had accomplished what no other woman athlete before her had done: she earned more than $100,000 per year. Babe had a good answer to why the big money came her way: "Where I go the galleries go." Yet even she was astounded by the sums of money. She once quipped, "Ah'm makin' it faster'n Ah can spend it." She never forgot her uncertain and impoverished youth, where a hamburger or even an orange was a luxury. "Where I go, these days, Ah gotta have mink," she said frequently.

Understandably, such proclamations prevented Babe from forming deep friendships with other women professionals. The one exception to this was Betty Dodd.

Betty was an excellent player out of San Antonio. Around the time she met Babe in 1950, experts believed she was the most promising young golfer of her day. Only twenty years old, Betty became infatuated with the star of the tour, and Babe took Betty under her wing. Almost instantly, Betty became Babe's constant companion. She recognized Babe's isolation. Babe did not have many friends nor was she terribly popular with her golfing peers. Dodd saw Babe's shortcomings, but she also saw what an extraordinary person she was. The loyal Dodd was enthralled with her idol.

By the end of the 1951 tournament season, Babe was fed up again with the endless traveling schedule, strange hotels, dreary food, and rootless lifestyle of a professional athlete.

She was famous, wealthy, bone-weary, and increasingly lonely. This time she was determined to go "home to pots and pans." Now, however, she wanted to include Betty Dodd in her plans. She asked Betty's father if his daughter could accompany her to Tampa so Babe could help Betty work on her game. He agreed and their bond grew from that point on. From their first meeting in 1950, until Babe's death in 1956, Betty was always at her side. Babe had finally found the devotion she needed. Now, she, Betty, and George would have to find a way to make a life together.

THIRTEEN

Choosing Family

B etty was fun-loving, energetic, physically fit, and possessed a charming smile, striking red hair, and freckles. She quickly became Babe's "running buddy," golf partner, domestic mate, and occasional confidante. Dodd adored Babe and reveled in the exciting life Babe led. "I never wanted to be away from her," Dodd once said. "I loved her. I would have done anything for her." Babe never publicly articulated her feelings for Betty this clearly, but she showed them. During Babe's lifetime, they never admitted that their relationship was also romantic and sexual, but it was, as Betty acknowledged years later.

In the 1950s, attitudes toward lesbian bonds were very hostile. It would have been professional suicide for Babe, Betty, or any women to publicly reveal their love for each other. Such an admission would have swiftly destroyed all the credibility and success Babe had labored more than twenty years to build. Not only were lesbians and gays not allowed in the military, they were fired from government jobs because people feared they were threats to national security. Psychologists labeled same-sex bonds deviant, and Americans believed what the medical profession told them. (The American Psychological Association did not change its official position until 1976, when it agreed that homosexuality was part of normal human relations.) Families frequently disowned gay and lesbian children and relatives, and churches excommunicated or shunned them. It was an environment that was not only negative for homosexuals, but also dangerous.

No wonder then that Betty and Babe deliberately chose to keep their relationship a secret. Neither they, nor George, nor the golfers and family members who knew of the situation spoke about Betty and Babe's love. Until Babe became ill, their relationship was either ignored or discussed in whispers. When average Americans thought about lesbians, they thought only about sexual relations—not about people taking care of each other every day. Babe and Betty feared they would be treated as outcasts if people found out about them.

Not surprisingly, when she dictated her autobiography in 1955, Babe played down her relationship with Betty. The book mentioned Betty only once, referring to her as "my buddy." Long before, Babe had learned the power the press possessed to make or break an athlete. She had no desire to subject Betty to the cruelty she had faced twenty years earlier.

The two were inseparable; nevertheless, their relationship was not an equal one. Wedged between them were the twenty-year age difference and Babe's worldwide fame, wealth, and forceful personality. But it was still a happy one because Betty did not insist that her career or wishes be taken as seriously as Babe's. Nor did she demand that Babe choose between herself and George.

Betty was never Babe's protégé, although stories saying so formed a rationale for their togetherness. Babe, according to Betty, simply was not interested in teaching Dodd to become a better golfer. Indeed, at times Betty's golfing excellence and fledgling fame irked Babe. However much she thought of Betty's talent, she was not willing to play "second fiddle" to another athlete. Betty's career never fully blossomed because of her devotion to Babe. She followed Babe everywhere, leaving little time for her own star to rise. Although she continued to compete, her game was not a priority. Betty was willing to make this sacrifice. Babe was worth it.

Betty accepted Babe's shortcomings gracefully. She was entertained by Babe's impromptu tap dances and shared Babe's love of Bebe the poodle and their music together. She never had any authority as manager over Babe as George did, so their relationship was not burdened by conflicting duties.

"Home" was the Tampa Golf and Country Club, which Babe had finally convinced George to purchase. The clubhouse was converted into living quarters, and Betty helped redecorate it. Babe adored it, naming it Rainbow Manor. In Tampa, they developed a comfortable arrangement. George had agreed to loosen control of Babe's earnings so they could purchase and maintain a home, but he was rarely there. His wanderlust was known by all. He would pack his suitcase, get in the Cadillac, and literally disappear. He claimed he was "seeing after his investments," but he also wanted to view the landscape and head to unknown places.

During his absences, Babe and Betty created a blissful domestic life together. In a real sense, Betty assumed George's former role. She catered to Babe's needs and took care of the demands of daily living. She also came to understand Babe's moods and vulnerabilities and respond to them helpfully. Betty understood Babe's decision to wear tailored shorts and shirts at home, but to appear feminine and dressy in public. She understood why Babe kept her Olympic medals stuffed in a coffee can on the kitchen counter and never discussed her track and field days.

Betty was aware that Babe's ego was behind her outbursts of temper when she lost. Betty did not compete with Babe for attention, as George had. Babe's choice to keep her marriage with George intact, or at least to make it appear as if the marriage were solid, was accepted by Betty as part of Babe's public image.

For George, the introduction of Betty Dodd into their married life and home was both infuriating and liberating. Betty relieved him of the marital responsibilities he did not want to fulfill. In fact, her presence allowed the marriage to continue. Without her, Babe would have fought with him more often. In addition, she would have been so lonely, she might have left George entirely. Betty was a sounding board for Babe and sometimes helped diffuse the tension between Babe and George. At other times, her presence produced friction, since Betty got the lion's share of Babe's attention.

Their marriage was stormy for other reasons too. George and Babe had never raised a child together, even though Babe loved children. She miscarried once, then wanted to adopt. George wouldn't hear of it, and their rift grew wider. Another area of contention was George's appearance. Her "Greek God" topped out at over 400 pounds. For Babe, who was always proud of her own fit body, this was embarrassing. Worse yet, his table manners were atrocious. His uncouth behavior haunted Babe. George had once been her greatest asset; now he had become a huge liability in Babe's quest to be socially accepted—even toasted—by the country club set. The final cause of disharmony between them was, ultimately, the most destructive. George did not listen when Babe complained of fatigue and pain. He wouldn't let her rest or slow down. If he had, it was possible she might have overlooked, even forgiven, his other traits that irked her. George continued to push Babe hard as her manager. In 1952, Babe was enjoying another stellar year, with Betty at her side. She had already won the Women's Titleholder's in March and the first two portions of the four-city Weathervane tournament. She led the LPGA in money winnings, again, by the end of April.

But her year was ruined when Babe developed pain and swelling in her left side. She couldn't seem to shake off the pain as she once had. In Seattle on the Weathervane tour, "those thirty-six holes were just agony for me," she said. Babe had withstood pain many times, and it was terrible for her to reveal it, but this was almost beyond endurance. She was forty-one years old, but felt sick and weak.

There are several versions about the events that happened next. George claimed he pleaded with her to see a physician. Dodd claims he pushed Babe to continue to the next tournament. Whatever actually happened, one thing is clear: George drove away in their Cadillac to escape the situation, and Babe drove with Betty as far as Salt Lake City, Utah. From there, incapacitated with pain, Babe flew to Beaumont to see Dr. E. W. Tatum.

The diagnosis was a strangled femoral hernia. Babe was

admitted to the Hotel Dieu Hospital immediately. The hernia had erupted, and it visibly protruded at the top of her left thighbone. It had stopped the circulation of the blood supply in the tissue. She also was anemic from overexertion. Babe's condition was critical. Tatum told her if she had waited another week, she might have "been a goner." Once she was strong enough, the two women returned to Tampa. With Betty's nursing, Babe recovered.

Babe returned to championship form by October 1952, to win the Texas Women's Open in Fort Worth. She also made a cameo appearance in the 1952 Hollywood film *Pat and Mike,* starring Katharine Hepburn and Spencer Tracy. The movie, in which Hepburn played a fabulous female athlete and Tracy her promoter, paralleled to some degree the life of George and Babe. The original script called for a golf scene showing Hepburn beating Babe, playing herself, by one stroke. Babe refused to be beaten. If she would not lose in real life, why agree to lose on film? Babe insisted that the script be rewritten so that she, not Hepburn, win by one stroke. It was. But despite this successful little foray into film, health problems intruded on her career. She only won four out of twenty tournaments. Furthermore, in her own mind, finishing in fifth place in money winnings with $7,503.25 meant a mediocre year.

At the end of 1952, Babe and Betty retreated to Tampa again. Babe was baffled about why she was chronically fatigued and suffered from bone-wrenching pain. Her golf game reflected her weakened physical condition. She would play a strong first nine holes of golf, then "run out of gas" as the match progressed. No amount of rubdowns ever relieved the muscle fatigue.

In March 1953, Babe wanted to make an excellent showing at the Beaumont Babe Zaharias Open Tournament, created to honor her. Mustering all her mental and physical
powers, Babe managed a one-stroke victory over Louise
Suggs when she made a birdie (one stroke under par) on the
final hole. It was a dramatic and emotional win, but Babe
nearly collapsed from the effort. She retreated to bed and,
cared for by Betty, anxiously waited for another appoint-
ment with Dr. Tatum the next morning.

During the months before this, Babe noticed she had
blood in her stool. She was vaguely aware that the blood
might be an early warning sign of cancer, but she kept
putting off facing the deadly possibility. The only person in
whom she confided was Betty. Babe decided to shield George
because they no longer spoke of intimate matters.

Her worst fears were realized when Dr. Tatum told her,
Betty, and George that she had colon cancer. As was the
common practice in those days, Tatum did not tell Babe how
bad her illness was. Physicians then believed if patients knew
the severity of their condition, it would hasten their deaths.
Tatum did tell George and Betty the grim truth: the cancer
was terminal. Babe was misled to think that surgery would
cure her.

FOURTEEN

A New Kind of Hero

Babe sat propped up in her hospital bed leaning against a bunch of plump pillows. The national press corps were crowded in the hallway of the Hotel Dieu Hospital in Beaumont, waiting to talk to her. Betty helped Babe comb her hair and apply fresh lipstick. Babe knew her picture would be printed nationwide, so she took particular care to look healthy and confident. The nation was watching her, and other cancer patients in particular would look to her example as a way of coping with their own disease.

Flowers and plants in vases from well-wishers filled the windowsill and perfumed the room. Her golf clubs, which Betty had hauled up into the room, stood bedside within Babe's reach.

The press corps flooded in. "Give 'em a smile," one journalist urged her, and she graciously obliged. It was a cheerful, animated gathering, complete with Babe's one-liners. She used sports metaphors to show how the disease was just one more challenge to overcome. Cancer, she said, is "the toughest competition I'd faced yet. I made up my mind that I was going to lick it all the way." Immediately after the operation, she decided that she was not about to let the illness "put me on the shelf." She had every intention of coming back and winning more championships.

She was putting on her bravest face for the world, but behind the bravado lurked despair. Other than her 1952 hernia operation, Babe had never been seriously ill. Her body had been a dependable, strong, and predictable ally. When her colon cancer was discovered, Dr. Tatum told her she had to have a colostomy to remove the visible cancer.

The prospect of the surgery made Babe despondent, as Dr. Tatum explained to her how different her life was about to become. During the operation, doctors removed all the cancerous portions they could find from her rectum and colon. Then they sutured her anal opening shut and rerouted her bowel so that her solid waste would pass through a permanent incision in her left side into a bag she would wear for the rest of her life. The bag needed to be checked and emptied frequently.

From the moment of the diagnosis, Betty moved into Babe's hospital room and stayed by her side. She slept on a portable folding cot and remained steadfast. Babe's surgery lasted more than four hours. April 17, 1953, was a grim day. The lead surgeon, Dr. Robert Moore, from the nearby University of Texas Medical Branch, and Dr. Tatum, Babe's personal physician, approached Betty and George in the post-operative waiting room. "She's got three strikes against her," Dr. Moore told them forthrightly. They had removed all the cancer in her colon, but they found rampant

Betty helping Babe exercise after her 1953 operation,
Hotel Dieu, Beaumont, Texas.

cancerous growths in her lymph nodes, which were spreading the cancer all through her body. There was nothing they could do.

George broke down and prepared to walk out. Betty asked Dr. Moore how long Babe would live. The colostomy would ease her pain temporarily, but he predicted the cancer would spread within a year and take her life. He counseled Betty and George not to tell Babe the wretched news. As Dodd recalled, "George was crying, I don't think he heard a word Moore said." George left. Betty tried to put the whole thing out of her mind and focused on cheering Babe. It was unthinkable for Betty that the invincible Babe, only forty-two, might be dying.

So, quite consciously, Betty and George helped create a charade for Babe: they never openly acknowledged to her that her condition was terminal.

With Betty's help, Babe began booking her own engagements. In 1953, shortly after her colostomy, the two women traveled to New York City so Babe could appear on the popular Sunday night variety hour, *The Ed Sullivan Show.* Originally, Babe was scheduled for just a walk-on appearance as a spokeswoman for cancer survivors. But she negotiated much more: a lengthy chat on camera with Sullivan while holding a golf club, and a musical number for herself and Betty on harmonica and guitar, as usual. This coup got her $1,500 and Dodd $350. Babe also booked two more appearances on popular television shows and acquired free music studio recording equipment, which she and Betty used to make a commercial record. She even arranged an impromptu jam session for the two of them on comedian George Jessel's show. Even when sick, she continued to be a tough negotiator.

Babe became a new kind of hero with her cancer battle. In the 1950s, cancer had a frightening stigma. Some people even thought it might be contagious. When someone received a cancer diagnosis, they often hid it from everyone they knew. Cancer was a disease people were ashamed of. Not Babe. She chose to "go public" in the hope of educating the American people.

She began her efforts even before her surgery. She announced to her fans that instead of flowers, they should send contributions to the Damon Runyon Cancer Fund. She had done benefits for this group years before. To her old friend, Tiny Scurlock, she said, "I'm tired of being on the sports page; put me on page one." He, and countless other reporters, did exactly that. By revealing that she had cancer and predicting she could "beat the disease," Babe gained a new degree of admiration. Now Americans viewed her as a brave, vulnerable, admirable role model.

She was extremely successful in publicizing cancer survival. The *New York Times,* for example, devoted far more coverage to her illness than it had ever given to her athletic achievements. In another irony, the presence of Betty Dodd was now widely recognized. Magazine and newspaper articles mentioned her as Babe's medical caretaker and loyal pal. In an interview with *Cosmopolitan* Babe said Betty was "steady as a rock."

Babe coped with her illness, and her recovery, in remarkable ways. From day one she was determined to save her career. Many people, such as her doctors and golfing peers, assumed that she would never again play competitive golf. Babe was determined to return. It seemed only Betty gave voice to Babe's dreams. "If it hasn't spread too far, you can play golf again," she declared. "You've got a chance, Babe."

As she prepared to get back into playing condition, Babe avoided getting too emotional about her situation. Throughout her life she had set seemingly impossible goals and used the lessons of sports to guide her. She saw her comeback as "the hurdle she could leap" and "the course she must run."

Babe's success had always come from pushing the limits of her endurance. She always strove for her "personal best" and public approval. This fight was no different. She began exercising on her own shortly after her surgery. Then, she astounded everyone by returning to competitive golf a mere fourteen weeks after her colostomy. In Chicago's Tam O'Shanter Tournament, she finished third, proving that she could be a contender again.

Encouraged by her Tam O'Shanter finish, Babe entered the Babe Didrikson Zaharias Week Golf Tournament in Beaumont in June. The Club, along with nearly 2,000 other courses, donated all proceeds to the Damon Runyon Cancer Fund. Babe won her hometown tournament.

Her swift return to championship form was rewarded when she was selected the Ben Hogan Comeback Player of the Year. She edged out baseball great Ted Williams of the Boston Red Sox, who had just returned from active military duty in Korea.

Babe requested that she be paired with Betty as a golf partner during tournaments. This not only boosted Babe's spirit, it also reassured her that Betty would be close at hand should any medical emergency arise. Ever the champion, she had one simple goal: to win. It wasn't enough just to compete, to get a respectable score, or to finish among the leaders. She needed to be first. "That's the standard I set for myself. I wouldn't want it to be any other way," she said.

But there were times that her physical difficulties overwhelmed her. During one month, she realized she couldn't sink the simplest putt. In despair, she sat on a bench, put her head in her hands and sobbed. Betty told her it was okay to quit. Just the mention of quitting snapped Babe out of it and fortified her resolve. With tears streaming down her face, she looked at her companion and exclaimed, "No, no, I don't want to quit. I'm not a quitter." Then she composed herself and began to hit like the Babe of old.

That year, 1953, was a disappointing one: she won only

two of twenty-four tournaments and was the sixth place money-winner. She had actually staged a tremendous recovery, but the goals she set for herself were so high that she could settle for nothing less than perfection.

That year she also seriously considered divorcing George. Rarely around, he still controlled Babe's money and hindered her decisions. Not only did George fear Babe's leaving, but he also worried that Betty would do Babe's bidding to arrange the divorce. "He got meaner than a snake," Betty recalled. Provoked by the possibility of a divorce, George vented his anger on Betty. "Me and Babe has been together and nobody's gonna break us up," he screamed at Dodd. Ultimately, Babe chose to maintain the status quo because of declining health and the years of familiarity she and George had together.

In her first few tournaments of 1954, she finished seventh, second, fifteenth, and third. Her frustration mounted. Babe knew fans wondered whether she could ever be capable of winning tournaments again, and in the ten months since her surgery, she was asking herself the same thing.

In February 1954, Babe's hard work and iron will paid off: she won the Serbin Women's Open, beating Patty Berg by one stroke with a par five on the final hole. This victory was the one of which she was most proud; Babe called it her "biggest thrill in sports." She had overcome pain, uncertainty, and doubting fans to reign as queen once again.

President Dwight Eisenhower and First Lady Mamie Eisenhower invited Babe to the White House. The president presented her with the American Cancer Society's Sword of Hope award. Babe immediately held the oversized sword like a golf club and took mock swings at imaginary golf balls. The award honored Babe's continuing efforts on

Babe mid-swing with George Zaharias looking on, at the first Babe Zaharias Open in Beaumont, Texas, 1953, a cancer fund-raiser.

behalf of cancer treatment. Equally important was the example Babe set as someone who could live with the aftermath of cancer and still have a full, productive life. The public knew her only as courageous and determined. When she was in the spotlight, she never showed her nagging worries that the cancer would return.

With Betty Dodd, Babe visited hospitals and strolled through cancer wards in various cities where they had tournaments. Playing harmonica and guitar, they cheered patients and gave them hope. With assistance, she personally responded to the hundreds, if not thousands, of letters that poured in from cancer patients. Babe said yes to every request for her help that would raise a dollar for cancer research or raise the nation's consciousness about the disease. She opened a Babe Didrikson Zaharias chapter of the American Cancer Society and made numerous personal appearances and radio and television pitches for cancer groups. Everywhere she went, Americans began to see her on two levels: as a champion athlete and as an exceptionally brave and giving humanitarian.

Her good deeds were complemented by a terrific year of golf in 1954. She won five tournaments, and she captured the All-American by eight strokes, missing her own course record by only one stroke. Babe phoned her physicians with news of her victories and attributed her comeback, in large part, to their skill. Moore for one retorted that "you did it yourself, Babe. It was your faith, Babe, that and your courage." Babe also credited others, including the thousands who had prayed for her. She had come to believe that prayer was a powerful ally.

She finished 1954 with second place earnings of $14,452. She was also awarded the Vare Trophy for having tallied the lowest scoring average. In April she received the William D. Richardson Trophy for "her outstanding contributions to golf within the past year." She also won the Serbin Trophy, newly created, which calculated high finishes in tournament play. For good measure, she was reelected president of the Ladies Professional Golf Association.

To complete her sweep of honors, the Associated Press voted her Female Athlete of the Year for the sixth time. No other athlete before or since has been so honored that many times.

Babe charged headlong into a golf controversy shortly thereafter. The golf equipment companies who refused to pay his salary any longer laid off Fred Corcoran, business manager for Babe and the LPGA. In support of Corcoran, Babe resigned as president of the LPGA in January 1954. Later that month, pro golfer Betty Hicks' article "A Lady Golf Pro Lets Down Her Hair: Next to Marriage We'll Take Golf" appeared in the widely read *Saturday Evening Post.* Hicks' article exposed some of Babe's less sensitive posturing, including her one-liners in the locker room, like "Why don'cha all go home?" Hicks also recounted the special treatment Babe received. Enraged, Babe made a big production of turning in her LPGA card in a press conference.

But Babe was a formidable opponent in the conference room as well as on the golf course. After she announced she was quitting, all-night negotiations ensued until Babe's demands, including the rehiring of Corcoran, were met. There was negative feedback from the Hicks article, but it was minimal because of her tireless efforts on behalf of cancer work.

Amid this turmoil, George decided they could build Babe's dream house, across the pond from the Tampa Golf Course club house. Babe affectionately called it Rainbow Manor. In March 1955, Babe, age forty-four, Betty, and George finally moved in. It was one of her life's great ironies that because her fading health and nagging fatigue forced her to withdraw more and more from cancer work and golf, she finally was able to live with George and Betty in the house she had coveted for so many years.

There were still tensions among the trio whenever George showed up. But at no time did Betty force Babe to make a choice between her and George. Since the two women were alone most of the time, Betty actually took over the role of spouse. Betty alone could cheer Babe out of the worst depression. As Babe's health dictated, Betty dutifully left celebratory parties, locker room chats, and social dinners, accompanying Babe home for an early night and rest. Betty was so competent that George became dependent on her too. He had developed diabetes. He was so afraid of Babe's illness that he could not care for her. Betty became more important than ever. "He was jealous of me," Betty said, "but as time went by ... he couldn't afford to be anymore."

Babe's health began its final downhill slide on a fishing trip with Betty and Betty's sister Peggy at Port Aransas, Texas. When their car became mired in the sand, Babe began digging it out with predictable ferocity. Pushing her body past its limit, she triggered a bone-deep pain, but she continued to compete. At the start of 1955, she won three tournaments and was reelected LPGA President.

At the Sea Island Invitational her stamina buckled. When she left the golf course lame and spent, she was rehospitalized and diagnosed with a herniated disc in her lower back, blamed on the digging. She was operated on to relieve the pain in June 1955. But unknown to her medical staff, the cancer had returned. Babe spoke of ongoing pain after the surgery. Because they could not "see" the cancer, some doctors thought her pain must be psychosomatic and they denied Babe much-needed pain medication. This level of vulnerability was maddening to Babe. Finally, one psychiatrist, Dr. Grace Jamison, believed her and ordered the medical team to reinstate her narcotics.

On Christmas 1955 Babe left John Sealy Hospital in Galveston to spend the holiday with her dear friends, the Bowens. They drove her to the Colonial Country Club to perk her up. It had been months since she had even seen the lush green rolling hills of a golf course. Babe bent down and put her hand on the warm tufted green, just feeling it.

It was her last contact with her beloved sport.

After months of agony, Babe was told on August 5, 1956, that her physicians had more evidence of cancer. Betty sensed that Babe was relieved. At least everyone now knew she wasn't imagining the pain. An innovative x-ray treatment aimed at lessening her discomfort was begun.

George, profoundly sad, told the press what they wanted to hear: "Babe took the bad news like the mighty champion she has always been," he said. "She's not giving up." Actually, because she had been led to believe that "they'd gotten it all" during her 1953 surgery, its recurrence crushed her. She was rarely public after that, although she did pose with her forty-fifth birthday cake at her hospital bedside. She looked gaunt, and it was clear her condition had deteriorated.

The very day her x-ray treatment began she finished dictating her autobiography. She kept up a brave front, predicting another comeback. "With the love and support of the many friends I have made, how could I miss?" she said. But even Babe hinted that she knew her future was bleak. "Maybe I'll have to limit myself to just a few of the most important tournaments each year," she wrote.

In her determination to overcome her illness, Babe was unequaled. However, as she refused to acknowledge her pain, emotional distress, and impending death, she was also an unrealistic role model. She created the expectation that other cancer sufferers should respond with the same stoic fight she had, which was unfair. Even Babe might have benefited from a more empathetic view of her illness. Had she spoken of her fears, memories, or love to either Betty or George, she might have permitted herself to receive emotional comfort from them. Three things prevented this: she, not George or Betty, was the strong, stoic one in her relationships; she wasn't aware of her true diagnosis; and in Babe's version of heroism, she could not admit frailty.

Babe was determined to leave a legacy as a humanitarian that rivaled her sports accomplishments. On September 12, 1955, from the sun porch at the Galveston hospital, she and George announced the establishment of the Babe Didrikson Zaharias Cancer Fund to help needy cancer patients. The first goal was to establish a tumor clinic at the University of Texas Medical Branch, the place where Babe's father had received free medical care.

Babe was rehospitalized in Galveston in December 1955 for one month; her pain was intolerable. After returning to Tampa, Babe harnessed her waning strength to go to Sarasota to watch Betty on the final hole of a tournament. Despite Babe's supportive presence, Dodd lost by one stroke. In March 1956, Babe asked to return to John Sealy Hospital; she never left there again.

With strong encouragement from Babe, Betty played in an LPGA tournament that June to honor Babe's birthday. It raised $5,000, which was donated to the cancer fund.

Within a couple of weeks, Babe underwent one final operation to relieve her pain. The press hovered. Indeed, at times the press coverage of her illness was so thorough it was invasive, almost carnival-like. But Babe chose to use her illness. She wanted to make cancer a household word for an American public that was terrified to mention it. Being famous was a role very familiar to her, and at this, her most difficult time, and she wanted the press to chronicle her now as it had all her life.

Despite her brave front, Babe died on September 27, 1956, at the Galveston hospital. Babe's brother, Bubba, as

Betty Dodd, George Zaharias, and Babe, John Sealy Hospital, University of Texas Medical Branch, Galveston, Texas, 1956.

she had requested, traveled with Babe's body to Houston for cremation. He brought her ashes back to Beaumont for burial in the Forest Park Cemetery. Her burial plot is across from the country club where she first played golf.

As Babe's inner circle grieved, the world's compliments rained down upon her memory. President Eisenhower paid tribute to her in a statement that hailed her athletic records and also noted, "in her gallant fight against cancer she put up one of the kind of fights that inspired us all." Babe's dramatic life had come full circle. She was a hero on every athletic field she ever set her foot upon—and she was a new kind of hero in death.

Today, we can imagine the twinkle in her eye as she surveys her burial plot. Well-meaning Beaumonters and family members had her gravestone inscribed with the message, "It's not whether you win or lose, it's how you play the game." With a chuckle, Babe probably would remind folks that a better epitaph might have been her often-quoted line: "I don't see any point in playing the game if you don't win, do you?"

Named the Associated Press Female Athlete of the Half Century in 1950, Babe departed with her image and astounding legacies intact. She forged new paths and wound up a national treasure. She never tried to be a role model for other women athletes, yet she has been an inspiration to countless women who came after her.

Her life was finally at an end. But not her legacy: that has a life all its own.

CHRONOLOGY

1911   Born Mildred Ella Didriksen, Port Arthur, Texas.

1928–30   Competed on Beaumont High's Royal Purple teams in basketball, golf, and tennis.

1930   Recruited by Melvin J. McCombs, the coach of Employer's Casualty Insurance Company (ECC), to play semiprofessional basketball, baseball, track and field, swimming and diving in Dallas; ECC wins AAU crown.

1930–31   Selected to the All-American basketball team with ECC; ECC wins national industrial league championship.

1932   AAU meet, Evanston, Illinois: doubled as tryouts for U.S. Olympic team. AAU and U.S. record: shot put (39 feet 6¼ inches); world record: baseball throw (272.2 feet); javelin (139 feet 3 inches); won 80-meter hurdles (12.1 seconds); AAU record tie high jump (5³⁄₁₆ feet); won broad jump (17 feet 6 inches); fourth in discus.

Los Angeles Olympic Gold in 80-meter hurdles; set world/Olympic record (11.7 seconds); won Olympic gold javelin; set Olympic and world record (143 feet 4 inches); won Olympic gold/silver in disputed high jump (5 feet 5¼ inches); voted Female Athlete of the Year by Associated Press.

1932–34   Babe performs in RKO stage show in Chicago; Babe resigns from ECC; pursues stunts and sideshows; pitches to major league hitters; performs boxing, football, billiards, basketball; travels with House of David baseball team.

1935   Ballyhooed exhibition golf tour with male pro Gene Sarazen; banned from USGA as a professional; meets Bertha and R. L. Bowen; the feminizing process begins.

1938   Meets George Zaharias at Los Angeles Open; engaged July 22, 1938; married January 3, 1939.

1940–42   Babe works at golf game; Zaharias supports them financially, retires from his own career, and manages hers with the goal of reinstating her amateur status; Babe masters tennis and bowling.

1945   Babe reenters top-level women's golf; wins her second Texas Women's Open Title; wins Western Open (third time); wins Women's Athlete of the Year from Associated Press poll (golf), second time for this award.

1946–47   Wins thirteen consecutive amateur golf tournaments; Babe signs with business manager Fred Corcoran; her endorsements begin; named Associated Press Woman of the Year, along with three other women.

1950   Voted Female Athlete of the Half Century by the Associated Press; cofounds the Ladies Professional Golf Association (LPGA) in New York; meets Betty Dodd in Miami; they return to the Zaharias' home in Tampa; 1950–1956, Dodd cohabitates with Babe and George.

1951   Inducted into Ladies Professional Golf Association Hall of Fame.

1952–56   Dodd becomes Babe's primary medical caretaker.

1953   Babe is diagnosed with colon cancer; operation
           results in colostomy; her remarkable recovery
           from surgery allows her to compete in a top-level
           golf tournament, Tam O'Shanter, where she fin-
           ished third only fourteen weeks after her surgery;
           founds Babe Didrikson Zaharias Week Golf
           Tournament; this begins her fund-raising and pub-
           lic appearances on behalf of cancer patients; wins
           Ben Hogan Comeback Player of the Year Award;
           voted Female Athlete of the Year by the Associated
           Press for the sixth time; reelected LPGA president;
           opens Babe Didrikson Zaharias Chapter of the
           American Cancer Society.

1953–54   Elected LPGA president.

1954   Awarded Medical Humanitarian Athletic Awards
           by American Cancer Society (1954) and Public
           Health Cancer Association of America (1956);
           Texas House of Representatives passes Resolution
           honoring her cancer crusade (1957).

1954–55   Reelected LPGA President.

1955   Babe, Betty, and George move into Babe's dream
           house, Rainbow Manor, Tampa, Florida; systemic
           cancer found.

1955–56   Repeated hospitalizations at John Sealy Hospital
           in Galveston, Texas; dictates autobiography, *This
           Life I've Led*, to Harry Paxton.

1956   Babe dies at University of Texas Medical Branch in
           Galveston, Texas, on September 26, 1956; buried
           in Beaumont, Texas.

POSTHUMOUS HONORS

1956	Won Graham McNamee Memorial Award, Greatest Women Athlete in History, voted by Sports Broadcaster Association; eighty-two golf tournament wins in eighteen years.
1974	Inducted into Track and Field Hall of Fame.
1975	Babe Didrikson Zaharias Memorial Museum opened in Beaumont, Texas.
1977	Inducted into Professional Golf Association Hall of Fame.
1981	Commemorative postage stamp issued.
1988	Player of the decade, 1938–1947, on the Centennial of Golf in America.
1990	Babe Zaharias Female Amateur Athlete Award honors top female athletes.
1999	Named *Sports Illustrated*'s Woman Athlete of the Century.
1999	Named the Associated Press Woman Athlete of the Century.
1999–2000	ESPN Television's "Sports Century: The Twentieth Century's 50 Greatest Athletes" lists Babe Didrikson in the top ten; she is the only woman selected in the top ten list.

SELECTED BIBLIOGRAPHY

Arnold, Peter. *The Olympic Games: Athens 1896 to Los Angeles 1984.* London: Hamlyn, 1983.

Banner, Lois W. *American Beauty.* New York: Knopf, 1983.

Cahn, Susan K. *Coming on Strong: Gender and Sexuality in Twentieth-Century Women's Sport.* New York: Free Press, 1994.

Cayleff, Susan E. "Babe Didrikson Zaharias: Her Personal and Public Battle with Cancer." *Texas Medicine Heritage Series,* vol. 82. Austin: Texas Medical Association, 1986.

Cayleff, Susan E. "The Texas Tomboy: The Life and Legend of Babe Didrikson Zaharias." *Magazine of History: For Teachers of History,* vol.7. Ann Arbor: Organization of American Historians, 1992.

Cayleff, Susan E. *Babe: The Life and Legend of Babe Didrikson Zaharias.* Chicago: University of Illinois Press, 1995.

Cayleff, Susan E. "Zaharias, Babe Didrikson (1911-56)." In *Handbook of American Women' s History,* ed. Angela Howard Zophy. Connecticut: Garland Press, 1990.

Corcoran, Fred. *Unplayable Lies: The Story of Sports' Most Successful Impresario.* New York: Meredith Press, 1965.

Crawford, Ann Fears, and Crystal Sasse Ragsdale, eds. "The Texas Babe." In *Women in Texas: Their Lives, Their Experiences, Their Accomplishments.* Burnett: Eakins Press, 1982.

Evans, Virginia Lou. "The Status of the American Woman in Sport, 1912–1932". Ph.D. diss., University of Massachusetts, 1982.

Gallico, Paul. *The Golden People.* Garden City, New York: Doubleday, 1965.

Gerber, Ellen W., Jan Felshin, Pearl Berlin, and Waneen Wyrick. *The American Woman in Sport.* Reading, Massachusetts: Addison-Wesley, 1974.

Gustaitis, Joseph. "Babe Didrikson: America's Greatest Athlete?" *American History Illustrated,* vol. 35, 1987.

Herndon, Booton. "I'm Not Out of the Rough Yet!" *Cosmopolitan,* October 1953.

Hicks, Betty. *Travels with a Golf Tour Gourmet.* Palo Alto, California: Group Fore, 1986.

Himes, Cindy. "The Female Athlete in America, 1860–1940." Ph.D. diss., University of Pennsylvania, 1986.

Howell, Reet, ed. *Her Story in Sport: A Historical Anthology of Women in Sports.* New York: West Point, 1982.

Kahn, Kathy, ed. *Hillbilly Women.* New York: Avon, 1972.

Johnson, William Oscar, and Nancy Williamson. *Whatta-Gal: The Babe Didrikson Story.* Boston: Little, Brown, 1975.

Lenskyj, Helen. *Out of Bounds: Women, Sport and Sexuality.* Toronto: Women's Press, 1986.

Linsley, Judith Walker, and Ellen Walker Rienstra. *Beaumont: A Chronicle of Promise.* Tyler, Texas: Windsor Publiciations, 1982.

Mrozek, Donald. "The Amazon and the American Lady: Sexual Fears of Women as Athletes." In *From Fair Sex to Feminism: Sport and the Socialization of Women in the*

Industrial and Post-Industrial Eras, eds. J. A. Mangan and Roberta J. Park. Totowa, New Jersey: Frank Cass, 1978.

Nelson, Mariah Burton. *Are We Winning Yet? How Sports Are Changing Women and How Women Are Changing Sports.* New York: Random House, 1991.

Roberts, Randy, and James Olson. *Winning Is the Only Thing: Sports in America Since 1945.* Baltimore MD: Johns Hopkins University Press, 1989.

Schoor, Gene. *Babe Didrikson: The World's Greatest Woman Athlete.* Garden City, New York: Doubleday, 1978.

Smith-Rosenberg, Carroll. "The New Woman as Androgyne: Social Disorder and Gender Crisis, 1870–1936." In *Disorderly Conduct.* New York: Alfred A. Knopf, 1985.

Ware, Susan. *American Women in the 1930s: Holding Their Own.* Boston: Twayne, 1982.

Zaharias, Babe Didrikson. *This Life I've Led: My Autobiography.* As told to Harry Paxton. New York: A. S. Barnes, 1955.

Zaharias, George. "The Babe and I." *Look,* vol. 88, 1957.

INDEX

ACKNOWLEDGMENTS

To Patricia Kelly, friend and children's literature maven, for her kind alertness in suggesting this publisher.

To Claudia Schaab, my first editor at Conari Press, for her perseverance and creative suggestions; and to Mary Jane Ryan and Heather McArthur, whose guidance took over from there.

To Grace Lichtenstein, editor par excellence, and co-enthusiast about Babe's life.

To the University of Illinois Press, for allowing me to make Babe's story available to another whole audience.

To Sue Gonda, whose encouragement, suggestions, incisive editing, word processing, and endless support made the summer months devoted to this project infinitely easier and laced with fun.

To Dawn Comeau, a gifted student and gracious friend, whose organizational help and dazzling attention to detail were a welcome relief and inspiration throughout the process.

To the staffs of the Babe Didrikson Zaharias Memorial Museum in Beaumont, Texas; the John Gray Library at Lamar University in Port Arthur, Texas; and the faculty and staff at the Institute for the Medical Humanities at the University of Texas Medical Branch, Galveston—all of whom were invaluable in the early phases of the adult biography.

And to Babe Didrikson Zaharias, for having lived a life that continues to inspire and confound.

ABOUT THE AUTHOR

Susan E. Cayleff is the department chair and professor of Women's Studies at San Diego State University in California. She is the author of *Babe: The Life and Legend of Babe Didrikson Zaharias,* for which she won the GLADD (Gay and Lesbian Alliance Against Defamation) Award for Outstanding Book; the book was also nominated both for a Pulitzer Prize and a Lambda Literary Award. Her other books include: *Wash and Be Healed: The Water Cure Movement and Women's Health;* and *Wings of Gauze: Women of Color and the Experience of Health and Illness.* In 1998, Cayleff was inducted into the National Women's History Hall of Fame in Seneca Falls, New York. She lives in San Diego, California.

THE BARNARD BIOGRAPHY SERIES

The Barnard Biography Series expands the universe of heroic women with these profiles. The details of each woman's life may vary, but each was led by a bold spirit and an active intellect to engage her particular world. All have left inspiring legacies that are captured in these biographies.

Barnard College is a selective, independent liberal arts college for women affiliated with Columbia University and located in New York City. Founded in 1889, it was among the pioneers in the crusade to make higher education available to young women. Over the years, its alumnae have become leaders in the fields of public affairs, the arts, literature, and science. Barnard's enduring mission is to provide an environment conducive to inquiry, learning, and expression while also fostering women's abilities, interests, and concerns.

Other Titles in the Barnard Biography Series